RESIDENTIAL SOCIAL WORK
*General Editor*: Tom Douglas

# Professional Supervision in Group Care

# Professional Supervision in Group Care

A CONTRACT-BASED APPROACH

*James S. Atherton*

## TAVISTOCK PUBLICATIONS

LONDON AND NEW YORK

First published in 1986 by
Tavistock Publications Ltd
11 New Fetter Lane,
London EC4P 4EE
© 1986 James S. Atherton
Typeset by Hope Services, Abingdon
and printed in Great Britain by
Richard Clay (The Chaucer Press)
Bungay, Suffolk

British Library Cataloguing in
Publication Data

Atherton, James S.
Professional supervision in group care:
a contract-based approach.—
(Residential social work)
1. Institutional care
2. Social service—Team-work
3. Supervision of social workers
I. Title    II. Series
361.4    HV59

ISBN 0–422–60420–8

For my parents
– my first 'supervisors'

# Contents

# Acknowledgements

In writing this book, I have become aware of two things above all: first, how easy it is to write so much about a fairly small topic, and how difficult to write so little; second, how much I owe to how many people for the ideas and the experience behind the book. There are far too many people to mention everyone, so I must just thank those who have had an immediate influence, and plead to the others that although space does not permit mentioning them by name, my appreciation is no less sincere.

Wives are conventionally acknowledged last, but in this case Susi has not only borne with my seclusion to write when I could have been putting the house to rights, but has also been a constant source of ideas, invaluable experience in residential work, and insistence that I keep my feet on the ground.

I must also acknowledge a great debt to all those who have taken part in short courses and workshops on supervision over the last ten years, and who have tested the ideas, criticized them, and raised questions that have led to their refinement. Thanks are also due to those who have worked with me in leading those courses, particularly David Bowdler and Doris Feak.

I owe much to colleagues who have suggested lines of thought and stimulated me in discussion: Doug Hearn, Peter Blackburn, and Arnold Critchley (now at Ardale) while at Salford; and Lynne Freeman, Janice Harper, Maria Ruegger, Maureen Sears (now at Ruskin College), and Andrew Sedgwick at Bedford. Outside the colleges, particular thanks go to Barbara Aldwinkle and Penny Forshaw for sharing their very different but equally skilful approaches to supervision.

For the writing itself: Peter Righton encouraged me to

write, Chris Payne of the National Institute for Social Work made detailed and very valuable comments on an earlier draft. Tom Douglas has been a very supportive and helpful editor. John Ericson of Bedford College helped to clarify many ideas on the theory of learning. Frances Hills typed the scruffy typescript on to disk, and without Chris Beeson's help it would never have made its way back on to paper again!

While all of these people deserve a share in any credit, the failings of what follows are entirely mine.

James S. Atherton
*January 1986*

# General Editor's Foreword

James Atherton starts his discussion of the supervision of those working in residential situations from an acceptance that it is a process not well founded in traditional practice and not even as well developed as the similar procedures in fieldwork. His intention is to create and maintain an interest and competence in supervision in group care specifically related to the needs of those working in that kind of system. But experience is, or can be, a good teacher, and Atherton is well aware of the formidable problems that group care offers to the establishment of a supervisory system; he minimizes none of them.

Mounting evidence suggests that social workers in general have a marked aversion to a process that in most cases has been a large part of their professional training. For some reason support systems like consultation, supervision, and self-reviewing groups are seldom used to any great advantage unless there is someone prepared to take the responsibility for setting up and maintaining the impetus of such a system. This tends to create the feeling that the idea of reviewing progress is not wholly acceptable. Review procedure is equated with pressure from an external authority.

Many factors may be involved in this aversion, not least of which may be previous poor experience of supervision. Although the direct correlation between feedback and quality of performance is acknowledged, at a rational level, to exist, there is considerable trepidation at the idea of involving oneself in it. I have a strong suspicion that this anxiety is related to two important points: firstly, a suspicion that feedback is criticism rather than a form of learning and may be an integral part of assessment from a promotional, disciplinary, or merit viewpoint; secondly, that it may be an unwarranted form of meddling in a form of work that is often manifested in a very personal way, whatever knowledge base it is founded upon.

James Atherton considers evidence that when workers discover how much effort has gone into a supervisory session there is generated a feeling that such a process must indicate a great lack on their part. However, he goes on to say that the act of supervision has more effect in its existence as a form of concern than in its execution as a technique, while hastening to add that concern which also takes the form of an efficient learning system is preferable.

I find myself in whole-hearted agreement with this approach. If anything comes across loud and clear from a long time spent working with groups it is the importance that group members attach to what is done. It is even more ephemeral than this, because it is not the actions themselves that count but the inferences made from them about intent. Concentration upon becoming a competent groupworker is good, but if it occurs at the expense of the perception by the group members that the intent is not one they are prepared to accept as viable, then it becomes a relatively sterile process. As this text clearly says, both the intent and method have to be appropriate to the situation.

In this context it is rewarding to find a writer who not only knows *about* supervision in group care, but who actually lives it and has the ability to write about it in a clear, direct, and punchy style. Atherton invites comment, even disagreement, with what he writes and does not make the elementary mistake of those deeply involved in their subject-matter of assumed omniscience. He talks to his reader directly, and openly states his bias and the reasons for it; parts of this book come as near as anything I have seen to a written form of tutorial or supervisory session.

As I have indicated, supervision tends to promote an emotional response that can and does obscure basic facts, like the discovery of ignorance clears the way for the beginning of learning. The admission of ignorance in our society brings about some considerable loss of self-esteem, and the pretence of wisdom is often deemed preferable, to the detriment of future learning. However, the amazing discrepancies that can be demonstrated to exist between self-assessed performance and the assessment obtained from involved others is a cautionary tale of great importance. Add to this that self-satisfaction can serve to eliminate even a hint of self-evaluation, and it becomes apparent that performance can remain static and even impervious to change in the circumstances in which it is being made.

It is thus doubly welcome that such a book as this should be written. Firstly, because it is aimed at a population where feedback of performance has seldom been growth-oriented and where encouragement to improve in work that is exhausting and intense is not often of sufficient strength or quality. Secondly, it is welcome because it is based in a philosophy which postulates not only that the development of those working in a caring situation is both acceptable and morally necessary, but also that it should be concerned with attitudes as much as, if not more than, with information and above all should not ignore the matter of competence.

There is much here that will be valuable to those not directly involved in group care, for in essence this is an essay in working with people.

Tom Douglas
*February 1986*

# Introduction

Field social workers tend to work on their own or perhaps with one or two colleagues. In particular, their encounters with clients are usually not witnessed directly by their seniors and managers. When they move beyond counselling and other enabling activities, and bring their authority and the wider resources of their agency to bear on a case, the consequences are often fairly dramatic; they may receive children or old people into residential care, they may provide respite care programmes, or arrange for domiciliary support of various kinds. Such arrangements commit expensive and scarce resources and therefore need to be sanctioned by the management of the agency. All these factors – the isolation, the invisibility of the direct work, and the potential commitment of resources – have contributed to the development of a structure and tradition of supervision by a senior worker, which monitors an individual social worker's case-load and the progress of each case.

Residential and day-care social workers, on the other hand, tend to work alongside their immediate managers. They have the opportunity to refer back to seniors in a matter of minutes if they encounter something out of the ordinary. They use their authority to intervene frequently in the lives of their clients, but they often do so in seemingly trivial ways: 'Yes, you can go down to the shops'; 'Come on, Mrs Jones, it's time for your bath.' Until recently, residential and day care have not in any case been acknowledged as part of 'mainstream' social work. For all these reasons, there has been no tradition of professional supervision.

Fieldwork supervision is often not as 'professional' in practice as its advocates would have us believe, and it suffers from many failings. So although supervision in residential and day-care settings has much to learn from the field, it needs to develop a distinctive approach that does justice to the setting, to the different demands on the staff, and to the situation of the clients. Practitioners are currently developing models of supervision drawn from many sources, but while fieldworkers have a relative wealth of literature to give them a basis for practice (Kadushin 1976; Westheimer 1977; and Pettes 1979 are amongst the best-known texts), residential and day-care workers have only pleas for more and better support (e.g. Berry 1975) or brief papers that are necessarily sketchy and not always easy to find (Hawkins 1982; Payne and Scott 1982). This book is one contribution to meeting that need.

The work leading to the book began ten years ago, when I started working with a small group of students on the old Certificate in the Residential Care of Children and Young People course at Salford College of Technology. Supervision for staff was then extremely rare, but both students and supervisors raised the question why permanent staff should not have the benefits of supervision that were enjoyed by students – who were in fact frequently more experienced practitioners than the majority of staff on their placements. These discussions led to a set of duplicated notes, which were later revised and used in a variety of settings, then to a programme of short courses in which I remain heavily involved, and to requests to put the material together in a book. This is the result.

## TERMINOLOGY AND ASSUMPTIONS

Defining terms is not a panacea, but it can avoid a degree of confusion as to the topic of the book. First, it is about 'professional supervision in *group care*'. This phrase has gained currency in Britain in the last few years, notably since the publication of Ainsworth and Fulcher's *Group Care for Children* (1982), where the reason for adopting the term is discussed. So far I have used the clumsy phrase 'residential and day care' to cover the same ground. But 'group care' is not only shorter, it also emphasizes two important principles: that clients are cared for *in groups*, *by groups* of staff. The fact that the clients constitute a group, with all the potential for good or ill that it implies, is frequently ignored. But whether we are talking about a day nursery or an old people's home, one of the most significant aspects of being a member of it is the continued presence of other people, and the sacrifices demanded and opportunities offered by this corporate experience. The dilemma of managing the interests of the individual and those of the group is also a central problem in day-to-day practice – and hence a continual issue in supervision.

Nor should the word 'care' be forgotten. If there is any sense in which residential and day care ever attains a degree of 'glamour', it is in the management of change in people – in their learning, development, achievement, or even 'cure'. While this should never be forgotten in those settings where such throughput is the aim, the essence of practice lies in the management of the hour-to-hour life-space of people who for whatever reason cannot do all the normal things for themselves. 'Care' focuses on this process, which can best be expressed in the words of William Blake: 'doing good in minute particulars'.

'Supervision' is, as far as this book is concerned, *the process of talking, to someone else involved in the same system, about what one is doing, in order to be able to do it better.*

*Super*vision is a problematic term, since it implies inspection from on high. One agency in a slightly different field prefers the term 'extravision', which avoids this and suggests a different pair of eyes looking from the outside at what one is doing. Preferable though this is in certain respects, it does not do justice to the important managerial component of supervision as we know it, and so I have stuck with the more usual term. 'Consultation' is another term used to cover the same ground as extravision, and Brown's book on this (1984) is a useful complement to this one.

'Supervision' is dealt with as having two aspects, which will be discussed in greater detail in Chapter 2: the *managerial* and the *personal/professional*. Clearly managerial supervision – in the sense of organizing staff to get the work done and providing the resources to do it – has always taken place. It is another way of saying 'management', and there is a great deal to be considered about how it may be tackled in group care, but this is not the place to say it. Managerial supervision is dealt with only in so far as it comes within the scope of a face-to-face supervision programme.

The professional aspect of supervision is concerned with enabling the particular staff member to perform as effectively as his or her capabilities permit within his or her defined role in the establishment. I refer to it above as the 'personal/professional' aspect because the staff member's major working resource is his or her *self* (and experience suggests that supervision is one of the most effective ways of freeing a staff member to use that self) – the personal touch and personal commitment that bring alive the process of caring (see Shaw 1974).

The subtitle defines the approach of this book as 'contract-based'. It would have been possible to produce an even-handed review of the different models of supervision on offer, and to leave it to the reader to sort between them. Instead, I have chosen to present all the ins and outs of one approach, which I believe to have proven value. You may wish to argue with me, and indeed I hope that you will, because that is a good way of clarifying your own ideas. Although I believe in this approach, the important thing is to find a way of working that fits a particular establishment and a particular staff team; and this can be found only by the practitioner on the spot. I think that the idea of a contract is the best guide to discovering this particular way. To change the analogy, a contract is far from a strait-jacket. It is a flexible device that calls for clarification of the objectives, nature, and progress of supervision.

In general, I have used the term 'clients' for the consumers of services. It is a term I do not much like, but 'resident' is too restricted (although I have used it occasionally for variety), because it excludes users of day-care facilities. 'Consumer' is both too vague and too passive for most contexts. 'Customer' is a useful corrective to 'client' – customers are always right, clients usually seem to be wrong – but at the time of writing it seems too flippant a term. I have referred to 'establishments' rather than 'homes' (or even 'Homes'), because the latter exclude day-care centres. The supervisor is sometimes male, sometimes female, but for the sake of clarity the supervisee is always of the other sex. I have used the term 'supervisee' only when it is really necessary for the sense or for emphasis, because being supervised is not the important thing about the staff member; what is important is her membership of the staff team and the work they do.

References to other writers in the text are made by citing the author's name and the year of publication of the work; full details are in the References at the back. But this is very selective – it does not constitute a guide to the literature on supervision or on contract-based work in other contexts. On the other hand, it does contain references to more general works which readers (perhaps mainly students) may wish to follow up because they stimulate thinking.

The underlying assumptions and theoretical background of the book come from systems thinking, in some of its many guises. Some of the ideas about communication, for example, owe much to Watzlawick, Beavin, and Jackson (1967) and to Bateson (1973); the approach to organizations draws on insights from Miller and Rice (1967), Miller (1976), and on their application to residential care in Miller and Gwynne (1972). Some of this thinking is readably summarized in de Board (1978). Supervision is seen, then, as an intervention in the life of an establishment that has a culture all its own, with its own checks and balances that keep it relatively stable from day to day. It is of the nature of any intervention in a system that it has indirect effects ('side-effects', if you like), as well as direct ones. I have tried to anticipate some of these, particularly in the sections that deal with problems. In other words, in social work nothing ever goes quite as it was planned to, and this is because of the enormous complexity of the people and systems involved. The situation is affected by everything from the economic and political system of the country to the unconscious motivations of individuals. The only chance of making an intervention work is to recognize such complexity, and systems thinking offers one of the best ways of doing this. However, this kind of systems thinking should not be confused with the more limited and specific 'systems approach' of Pincus and Minahan (1973).

Particularly if supervision is new to an establishment, it fits with the general model of planning an intervention shown in *Figure 1*. (For a more general discussion of this kind of process, see Carter *et al*. 1984.) The model shows that each phase affects those that follow it, and *should* be affected by them in turn through the process of feedback – although this can be blocked. If an intervention does not 'work' – whatever that means in its particular context – it may be the fault of any of the phases, and so this book tries to look at all of them in relation to supervision, but necessarily concentrates on those within the 'intervention' boundary. But the proof of the pudding is in the eating, and the ultimate evaluation must take place in relation to the task of the establishment (leaving aside that of the agency and its appropriateness in the social structure as a whole). The focus of the book is therefore on saying 'if supervision is an appropriate intervention, this is a

*Figure 1* Basic planning model

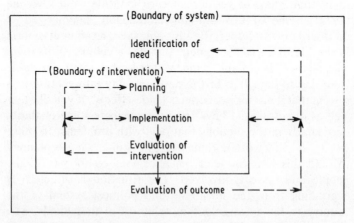

*Note*: Solid arrows show initial sequence of events; broken arrows show feedback processes

way of going about it'. As the chapters on 'Preparing for Supervision' (Chapter 3) and 'Introducing Supervision' (Chapter 9) suggest, other factors may be more important at this stage in an establishment's development. Social workers' mistakes are often mistakes about the boundaries of the systems in which they intervene.

THE PLAN OF THE BOOK

The structure of the book broadly follows the sequence of the planning model above; it begins with design, proceeds to implementation, and then looks at issues that may be raised by feedback and evaluation procedures. The book is in three parts, therefore. The first seven chapters set out the basic considerations of a supervision programme; Chapter 8 deals with topics for discussion in supervision; and the remaining chapters look at specific issues that may cause problems or require a special approach. To use the book as a textbook for supervision practice, the first part may be taken on its own; the second and particularly the third parts may be returned to when the practitioner has acquired some experience and confidence (although Chapter 9 will be found useful at an early stage if supervision is an innovation).

Chapter 1 is about what supervision should and should not be expected to do. As the planning model suggests, there is no point in setting up a system to do something it was never intended to be able to do in the first place. Although supervision can achieve many things and contribute to the achievement of practically any kind of practice one cares to mention (including bad practice), it is not a panacea. Readers using or contemplating supervision systems may find it useful to make a note of their aims before reading this chapter, to check the fit between what they are hoping for and what supervision can reasonably be expected to achieve.

Chapter 2 considers forms of supervision and comes down in favour of a formal system. This is one of the situations where formality paradoxically widens the scope of something rather than narrows it. Some of the issues to do with the introduction of a formal system are mentioned briefly in this chapter, to be picked up in greater detail in Chapter 9.

Chapter 3 looks at the foundations of a successful programme, in terms of the requirements that need to be met before it can flourish. Supervision *can* be carried out without them, but to try it is to invite problems on which it may founder.

Chapters 4 and 5 focus on the contract. Although contracts are finding their way into several forms of social work, they are still sufficiently unfamiliar to require a fairly detailed introduction. The contract is also the distinctive feature of the approach I am putting forward, and as such it has implications for the conduct of most aspects of the supervision programme, so these are explored.

Having set out the framework for supervision, Chapter 6 concentrates on the course of the sessions themselves, both within each session and over a period. Chapter 7 completes the overview by putting forward some ideas on recording and monitoring the supervision process, both as a feature of the life of the establishment and in terms of the development of the individual staff member.

Chapter 8 forms the second part, and provides guidelines for the discussion of several common topics in supervision: incidents, individual clients, the effects of clients on each other, routines, staff roles, theory, and facts.

Chapter 9 introduces Part Three, by returning to supervision as an instance of innovation in a group-care establishment and thereby raising more general considerations about change, which can be applied in many other areas. One of its main messages is to take objections seriously; and the chapter attempts to embody this in its own approach, with a sympathetic discussion of various reasons for *not* supervising.

Chapters 10 and 11 concentrate on two more subtle features of what goes on in supervision: roughly the counselling and educational elements. Both are present in supervision all the time, even when the main focus is managerial; and whatever the main focus of the programme, it is enhanced by taking these elements seriously.

The book concludes with a brief consideration of two

specialized forms of supervision: student supervision and group supervision. The latter in particular raises a number of complex issues that cannot be discussed in detail, but some pointers are offered towards the fairly advanced technique of the supervision of groups.

At one time I was convinced that supervision was *the* key to the improvement of practice in group care. I no longer make such grandiose claims, but experience in working with more than two hundred present and potential supervisors has taught me that it is not only what goes on in the sessions themselves that makes the difference. It is also what supervision *represents* – a concern for staff members as people, a preparedness to listen to them and to move towards greater autonomy for them and respect for their professional practice. As in all other aspects of group care, technique is less important than the values that underpin it.

# Part One

# 1 Aims and Objectives of Supervision

Professional supervision is not a cure for all ills, nor is it a specific for certain problems in residential practice. It is, however, a means of improving the overall health of an establishment, if we follow Nietzsche's definition of health as 'the ability to overcome disease'.

It is *not a substitute for training*. Much of the value of training courses comes from exposure to other course members with other experiences and other ideas, and from the opportunities presented by such exposure to clarify one's own ideas. Going away from the unit to college, if only for a day a week, also helps a staff member to gain some psychological as well as physical distance from immediate working problems, and that is hard to achieve in the unit itself. Training also covers wider issues than there is time for in the unit. But supervision does complement training, and indeed it is very important in that capacity.

The transfer of ideas from college to work is difficult, partly because it is sometimes hard to see their direct applicability, partly because practice is so much dirtier than theory, and partly because one might not think that there is scope in one's present position to try things out. The major training programmes have recognized this, and study supervision (which is professional supervision with the agenda set by college work) is a requirement on both the In-Service Course in Social Care and the Certificate in Social Service. CQSW students of course have supervision on their placements, but they are frequently presented with a massive problem when they return from their block away from work – in part how to be re-assimilated into the life of the unit, and in part the transfer of learning. Some students just cannot afford to change, because to do so would make it impossible for them to return to their previous posts; and since in many cases they are long-established residential workers, with houses on campus and growing families in schools in the area, it is easy to see that they are costing things out very realistically.

With the assistance of supervision, there is a chance that they might be able to apply their learning. The sheer existence of a supervision programme testifies to the commitment of the establishment to staff development, provides a listening ear for anxieties, and helps them to feel that they are not oddities out of their place. Good supervision can also help them to work through their fantasies about 'nothing ever changes in this dump', and to clarify what they can try out and what not. It can also help towards a realistic appraisal of the training experience, rather than the idealization or denigration in which so many indulge. (Such extreme views are often the expression of 'cognitive dissonance'; see Festinger 1957 and many others since.)

So if supervision does not replace training, it does protect the training investment. What is more, in conjunction with staff meetings, it can make a contribution to the solution of a training problem that applies particularly to group-care settings. This is that it is very inefficient to take one or two people out of an establishment, train them, and then feed them back and hope that anything will change. The pressure of the way things are already seen and done is almost bound to be too much.

Every year for about six or seven years there were two students seconded on to the course from one large establishment. So, even allowing for staff turnover, there was a higher proportion of qualified staff in that establishment than in any other in the region; and it made not a blind bit of difference to what went on there. Regardless of anyone's intentions, the piecemeal training of individuals was not sufficient to effect change in the organization as a whole. The only complete solution to this is to be found in an integrated programme of development and training that involves all the staff, but supervision and staff meetings can help.

In the section on staff meetings (pp. 27–31) I mention the principle of representation; it helps both the staff member on a course and his colleagues back home to get the most out of training if the 'student' sees himself, and is seen by colleagues, as attending on their behalf as much as on his own. While the most direct way of facilitating this process is giving time in staff meetings for reporting back on the course and perhaps performing some exercises arising out of it, an important indirect complement to this is working in supervision to ensure that other staff are ready to work with what their colleague brings back with him.

Supervision is not a substitute for staff meetings; see Chapter 3, 'Preparing for Supervision'.

Supervision *cannot mould people into the kind of staff you want*. Fortunately staff come in all shapes and sizes, and they tend to have their own ideas. Such diversity, if harnessed, is very good for any establishment. But if staff selection is a mess in the first place, it is no good relying on supervision to turn a sow's ear into a silk purse (or vice versa). Supervision can help diffident staff to become more confident. It can help abrasive staff to tone themselves down. But it cannot, and should not be expected to, overturn strongly held beliefs, values, and life-styles. If it does appear to be succeeding in this, be careful to monitor what is happening in the staff member's practice; it is probable that she is just going along in the sessions and going her own sweet way when the supervisor is not looking (see Chapter 11, 'Learning and Change').

*Supervision cannot replace good management*. If the unit is managed properly, supervision will complement an appropriate structure with the appropriate personal practice, which will make the whole thing work. If the unit is not managed properly, you can supervise until you are blue in the face and that of itself will not provide the appropriate structure. Management in a residential establishment has to define the task, and to hold the boundaries in such a way that those working within them are given the maximum space and freedom to work (whether they are residents or staff). (For further elaboration of this idea, see Miller and Gwynne 1972.) The sheer existence of supervision sessions may symbolize part of this framework, but more important are efficient procedures for ordering and buying, equitable staff rotas, the sensitive management of routines, and effective liaison with the agency and the community. These are never perfect, of course, and waiting until they are perfect will ensure nothing else ever gets done at all; but it is important that they should be good enough.

Supervision can help all staff (including the supervisor(s)) to break out of ruts. It can contribute to the application of 'treatment plans'; it can encourage creativity and confidence; and above all it can free staff members to engage with the residents as people, using their *selves* instead of merely a battery of techniques, recipes, and defences.

## ON OBJECTIVES

'Aims and objectives' is a phrase that crops up time and again in material on education, training, and staff development, and the words tend to be used as if they were synonymous. They can be interchanged in many cases, but whereas the overall aim of supervision may be expressed vaguely as 'to improve the quality of life of consumers of our service by enhancing staff performance', the practical objectives will necessarily be more limited. Objectives should preferably be linked to recognizable outcomes. Such outcomes are not necessarily behavioural (although some hard-liners would argue that they must be; see Mager 1962), but they do need to be fairly specific.

On many training courses, notably the CSS, efforts are made to specify in advance what the objectives are for all participants, and such an approach has great value in clarifying what a course is supposed to achieve. However, it cannot be applied to professional supervision because it rests on the assumption that someone, somewhere, knows precisely what is needed in order to be able to do the job effectively, and the task of training (or supervision) is to raise the student (or staff member) to that level. Supervision does not rest on that kind of 'deficiency' model of the supervisee, but more on co-operation between supervisor and staff member to help both (but mainly the staff member) to 'raise their game'.

On the other hand, supervision cannot be carried out effectively if neither supervisor nor staff member has a clear idea of what the desired outcomes are. It is therefore necessary to specify, individually, the objectives for each staff member taking part, so that even in the first supervision session there is a basic framework and sense of direction for the work. The following discussion is intended to provide some tools to clarify aims and objectives in setting up supervision. Further detail on working out objectives for individual staff members will be found in Chapters 4 and 5.

LEVELS OF SUPERVISION

There are two major levels of supervision: the *institutional* and the *personal/professional*. (For other ways of subdividing the topic, see Caplan 1970; Kadushin 1976.)

**The institutional level**

This is the level that overlaps most with the managerial function of the Head of Home, and the tensions involved in this are discussed elsewhere (p. 120). At this level, supervision is concerned with working with one staff member to find out how she is taking up her role within the formal structure of the unit, and how management can organize the unit or a particular aspect of her work in such a way as to give her the maximum space to do her job effectively. This comes down to:

(1) Induction: making sure that individual staff are familiar with establishment policies and why they work as they do.
(2) Getting reactions: to what it is like to put these policies into practice face to face with the residents.
(3) Feedback: giving a chance to voice grumbles and dis-contents directly to someone who can do something about

them (rather than grumbling to colleagues for the sake of it), and a chance to communicate new ideas, plans, and proposals.

As the above list shows, institutional aspects of supervision are not one-way communication. Equally important is what comes back from the staff member. On the whole, this kind of material may be expected to occupy about a quarter to a third of the supervision session, although it will be more with new staff and perhaps when supervision is just starting (especially if one starts by going through the job description). If it regularly takes up more time than that, it is worth wondering why. Is it because discontent with management is so important that it is blocking everything else? Or is it because other forms of management communication are not adequate? Or is it a cover for other things, a way of avoiding personal and professional issues? The fear of self-exposure can lead both partners to collude in that kind of avoidance.

### The personal/professional level

'Personal' and 'professional' are here used together as an acknowledgement that the worker's self is the most important tool and resource he has in social work. One of the costs of the increasing rhetoric of 'professionalization' in residential work has been the effective downgrading of other things that the practitioner has to offer. Professionalism can be used as a defence against personal involvement; and if it is ever separated from the personal touch, it *will* be used that way. Supervision is directed in part at helping staff to effect a continuing union between their personal and professional selves. On the other hand, if we concentrate exclusively on the personal side and ignore the professional, the supervision becomes a counselling session. It may be important for staff members to be largely freed from personal anxieties and problems originating outside work so as to be able to make themselves available to the residents, but supervision is concerned only incidentally with such matters. Supervision takes place for the benefit of the consumer, not for that of the staff member.

Personal growth for the staff member is an almost inevitable side-effect of good supervision; but particularly in more 'therapeutic' units, and where the clients do not seem to want to be treated, there is a temptation for staff to displace their aspirations to psychotherapy on to doing it to each other. This needs to be watched.


SUPPORT AND CHANGE

Within both the institutional and the personal/professional levels, there are two other strands to be distinguished. Part of the task of supervision, most supervisors would agree, is to enable their colleagues to carry on working effectively when the job and the circumstances are stressful, depressing, and even frightening. This is supervision for *support*.

On the other hand, no staff member is perfect, and much supervision is directed at getting them *to change*, whether in terms of correcting particular failings in practice, or generally encouraging more insightful, sensitive, and effective work.

One major challenge of supervision is to balance these two demands, and to adjust the relationship to accommodate them both. Supervision for support may be seen as a warm bath – soothing, relaxing, and refreshing. Supervision for change is more like a cold shower – bracing, awakening, and sometimes shocking. The two forms are difficult to accommodate within the one session and the one relationship, and we shall return to the tensions involved at various stages later. Nevertheless, both of them are necessary, and compromise does not work; a tepid bath or shower is a sorry thing. 'How I wish you were either hot or cold! But because you are lukewarm, neither hot or cold, I will spit you out of my mouth' (Revelation, 3:15–16).

# 2 Strategies of Supervision

'Strategies' is a rather grandiose term to use, but this chapter is concerned simply with organizing the practice of supervision so that it both has a chance to be effective, and does not conflict too much with all the other things that go on in a residential establishment, which may realistically have a prior claim on your time and that of your staff.

## INFORMAL SUPERVISION

Like the Molière character who discovered to his joy that he had been speaking prose all his life, informal supervision is practised in most establishments, although it is often not recognized as such. It consists of quick chats with staff members, either in the presence of the clients or of the 'Could I just have a quick word with you in the office?' style. Very often such encounters are simply about decisions that have to be made, or need to be communicated, and as such they are necessary and taken-for-granted parts of the management system. The introduction of a more formal supervision system would make no difference to these meetings. Sometimes they are also used to pick up on aspects of staff practice that deserve comment; and this is where they become part of informal professional supervision. Unfortunately, I suspect that most of the things picked up in these brief chats are the bad bits of practice, and staff come to think of being asked to step into the office as an occasion for being 'told off'. So if one is thinking of building on an existing informal supervision 'system', the first thing to do is to make sure that it covers more than crisis intervention when staff are doing things wrong or causing problems for themselves or others.

Informal supervision has the great advantage of *immediacy*. The supervisor can pick things up almost at the moment that they happen, comment on them, discuss them with the staff member, and then return the staff to the fray even before the incident is over. It is very useful for inexperienced staff who need to learn to pick up how trends within the group are developing, or for helping them to see the effects of a particular working style on a particular person. Because the 'raw material' is so close to hand, the learning can be dramatic.

The disadvantage of informal supervision is that, although it is easy to practise, it is extraordinarily difficult to do *well*. It requires tremendous discipline on the part of the supervisor to use it for anything other than crisis intervention, and for positive support it often seems perfunctory or even sarcastic. For example: Senior staff member passes through the lounge after tea, claps junior staff member cheerfully on the shoulder and says, 'Keep it up, you're doing a grand job!' Junior is left feeling, 'Oh, if you only knew the half of it . . .' or 'What do you mean by that?'

Then there is the question of how one builds on informal supervision and makes more use of it than at present. How much time can and should staff members spend being snatched out of situations in order to be supervised? Once in the office, there is rarely time to talk through an issue properly, and the supervisor tends to be in control of this indeterminate time, so that there is little chance for the staff member to come back at him. As soon as he has said his piece, he says, 'I think you ought to be getting back now.' Whether the staff member stays or goes, she loses something. Informal supervision is essential, but it is limited when used on its own; it can also breed resentment among staff and increase their sense of distance from their seniors, rather than weld them into a working team.

FORMAL SUPERVISION

At the other end of the scale is the practice of having formal supervision sessions with staff, with time set aside for a regular period at predetermined intervals, such as an hour a week.

The great advantage of the formal session is that it allocates a period of time that both parties know is concerned exclusively with supervision. For the reluctant supervisor or supervisee the very existence of the hour demands that work be done. More than that, the existence of the clear boundaries of the session means that there is a degree of security for both sides. The supervisee should be able to know that his supervisor will not be distracted by having other demands made on her, and she can be sure that there will be time to follow issues through.

The big disadvantage is the time-consuming commitment of formal supervision. With the best will in the world, and taking full advantage of the greater opportunities for delegation afforded by having a supervised staff team, the fact remains that finding sufficient time when it is mutually convenient is a perpetual problem. (For further discussion see Chapter 9, 'Introducing Supervision'.)

There are several practical solutions. The supervision can be shared amongst a number of staff, so that each has to find time for only two or three sessions a week; or a 'cover' system can be devised to ensure that people are not interrupted, perhaps by scheduling supervision when shifts overlap at change-over. As usual it is a question of priorities (see Chapters 4 and 5 on the supervision contract).

Formal supervision also makes more explicit demands on both parties (especially when there is a formal contract). There will be rough patches in any supervision relationship when the participants spend their time sniping at each other, or talking about neutral and non-threatening things, and when it seems that in view of the cost in terms of time and effort it would be better to give up (see p. 69). In this case, the existence of a formal commitment gives some incentive to work through the rough patches and to make sure that the time is not wasted.

The planned time commitment is just the tip of the iceberg of formal supervision. The remarkable thing about a formal set-up is the way in which holding firm such external boundaries gives freedom within them; both the cold shower and the warm bath can be accommodated. Informal supervision should be more appropriate to the warm bath (after all, subcultural peer-group support rarely offers anything else), but as I have suggested, in practice it is used more for the cold shower.

## INDIVIDUAL AND GROUP SUPERVISION

Group supervision has a chapter to itself later on (Chapter 13). These remarks intend only to make the distinction in terms of task between the two methods. Supervision *in* groups is simply a way of conducting professional supervision that is more economical on senior staff time, but supervision *of* groups really needs an individual supervision programme as well if it is to yield all its fruit. The two approaches also achieve different results.

Individual supervision concentrates on the development of personal practice in a way that might be threatening if carried out within a group. Group sessions work on the contribution of the team as a whole to the task of caring for the residents, and focus on individuals only in terms of their membership and role within the overall team structure. At a simple level, if a staff member has become a 'baddy' in the eyes of Johnny, while a colleague – who may be much less experienced and even less competent – is Johnny's good object, then the consequent tensions can be properly worked through only in the group as a whole. Both staff members need to be aware of the value of their own contributions, and helped to work together in such a way that the split is not reflected in their own relationship. This is one example of a much more complex structure whereby the tensions and difficulties within the staff group either reflect or are reflected by similar tensions and difficulties within the group of residents. No individual supervision session can really get at such issues; and indeed, because in an individual session the supervisor is working primarily with one person's account of what is going on, there is a danger of making the situation worse rather than better.

On the other hand, if one is working with a staff member on her own it is easier to start from where she is. In the group, that starting-point can easily be confused by the differing levels of experience, expertise, and confidence amongst the members – particularly as these relate to working in groups. And in some cases the effect of this confusion can be to send group supervision way off course. In one instance the supervisor was an outsider and he was simply not told the whole truth about what was going on in the establishment. There were complex reasons for this, but if he had seen all the members of staff individually, he and they would not have got caught up in a consensus, or even conspiracy, to ignore very important information, which was a perpetual topic of conversation amongst the staff on their own.

In an individual session, it is possible to spend time with an inexperienced member of staff looking at the 'silly things' that clients get upset about, which are not at all 'silly' to the clients themselves. In another session on the same day, the supervisor may be working with a more experienced member of staff on the family dynamics that might account for Johnny's hostility to male members of staff when he returns from visits home. In a group, it would be difficult to tackle either issue without either boring or losing some members of it.

# 3  Preparing for Supervision

This chapter is about clearing the ground. There are many features of residential and day-care work that are the province of management rather than of professional supervision, and so this section is designed to provide a concise check-list of things to pay attention to before starting on supervision proper. Without such preparation, related topics will keep coming up again and again in supervision sessions and will have to be dealt with then, which is frustrating because they hinder the real work.

## JOB DESCRIPTIONS

In order to supervise someone's work, one needs to know fairly accurately what that person can and cannot be expected to do. Job descriptions are limited tools, because they present a static snapshot of what someone's job looks like at a particular point in time; but they are useful because they provide a base-line for the assessment of change – change not only in the practice of the individual, but also in the demands being made on him.

For junior posts in residential care (Grades 1 and 2 in residential care), many agencies have a standardized job description, which applies regardless of the particular home the applicant is going to work in. Since in many local authorities the practice is to appoint staff technically to the department as a whole rather than to a particular establishment – in the interests of being able to move them if necessary – this kind of job description is necessarily generalized and vague. It is good practice to draw up more specific job descriptions to use when interviewing candidates for a job. For supervision purposes, too, such more precise and detailed job descriptions are highly desirable.

Moreover, it is important for supervision purposes to pay attention not only to the formal components of the job, which all Grade 2 staff may share in common, for example, but also to the informal elements. If it so happens that Dave does the majority of the minibus driving, make a note of that. If Chris trained as a confectioner before coming into social work and bakes all the birthday cakes, include that too. In supervision different roles within the overall staff team are as important as the common role of Residential Social Worker (see Chapter 13, 'Group Supervision').

One of the early supervision sessions may be devoted to going through the job description and checking out its accuracy. In fact, it is a useful exercise for the supervisor and the staff member to write a job description each (preferably following a similar format) so that the final products can be compared. This can easily yield a great deal of information to get supervision off to a good start.

Job descriptions for more senior posts are often more problematic, and even the written ones may fudge important issues. Take a common phrase like 'to deputize for the Unit Leader in his absence'. It is not clear from that kind of phrase just what are the limits of the discretion of the Deputy Unit Leader to whom it applies. At what point does he feel that he has to go and consult someone else? Has he the authority to make exactly the same kind of decision as the Unit Leader when he is not there? If so, given that the Deputy Unit Leader works on an opposite shift, and the Unit Leader works a 38-hour week, what makes one into the leader and the other into the deputy? What are the critical points, or thresholds, at which the difference shows? Supervision is likely to show up confusion and anomalies in such matters, and it helps if they can be clarified at a structural level beforehand. (They will almost certainly change over time, but supervision can monitor the changes and clarify them.)

Let us go further. What is the basis on which authority is distributed within the establishment? Is differentiation founded on having authority only over a sub-group within the whole? This is what the job titles in some large establishments imply, but they are not always realistic when it comes to how things work out in practice. Is it based on having authority to make decisions about a client only in a certain limited context? Is it based on the length of time for which a decision is likely to affect a resident? Staff often find out the extent of their authority only when they exceed it and are picked up for it; but for realistic supervision, it is important that the boundaries of authority are spelt out so that it can be established that the person fits effectively with the role. Although organization studies can be helpful here, they sometimes fail to do justice to important aspects of reality, such as the fact that the Head of Home lives on the premises and is relatively accessible even off duty, or even that the strata of the hierarchy are effectively separated by a system of master and sub-master keys that limits the access of junior members of staff to progressively fewer areas of the building and fewer resources.

To put it simply, in supervision you cannot criticize someone for not filling or exceeding their role unless it is clear what that role is.


STAFF MEETINGS

Offering individual supervision without having staff meetings is a recipe for manipulation. If it works, which it rarely does, it leads to the situation where the supervisor sits like a spider in the middle of her web, receiving vibrations from all points of the compass, and hence the maximum amount of information – whilst ensuring that others on the periphery do not communicate with each other at all. The scope for manipulation is obvious. In fact, in those settings where one person undertakes the supervision of everyone else, this pattern is endemic. It therefore needs to be countered by a regular programme of staff meetings, designed to keep everyone in the picture about important developments, and to ensure that there is a properly constituted forum where staff can talk to each other about problems.

Staff meetings in residential establishments are notoriously difficult to arrange so that everyone can be present. Rotas have to be twisted and pulled to cope with shifts and days off and day release for in-service courses, and so on. Most establishments, however, seem to manage to find a regular time at least once a fortnight for all the staff to sit down together and to face each other. The principal exception is the old people's home, which has a large number of part-time care assistants with other commitments (for more detailed discussion of this issue see Chapter 13, 'Group Supervision').

Staff meetings have many functions, of which the two clearest are to do with their technical and social sides.

**Technical**

Practices differ in varying settings, and although some are better than others most are probably good enough. It is worth mentioning, however, what the staff meeting has to be able to do in order to provide a sound foundation for supervision.

(1) The staff meeting needs to keep people informed. The better informed everyone is, the less likelihood there is of rumour and fantasy dominating the internal life of the staff group. For supervision purposes, it is a great help – and time-saver – if you can be sure that every member of staff has received and understood the same information in the same way.

(2) It needs to be a forum where any staff member's ideas and complaints can get an airing. As will become apparent later, there are occasions in supervision when a member of staff has to be told that supervision is not the best place to raise an issue, and that it should be taken to the staff meeting. Unless there is a forum prepared to hear the staff member, this does not make sense. The session needs to be a staff *meeting*, not merely a Head of Home's briefing.

(3) It needs to have some power, if only power to advise and consent. However the limitations on the authority of the staff meeting are set, it needs to be clear to all concerned

that decisions made within the boundaries of that authority will be respected by everyone, including the Head of Home. Unless this is seen to be the case, staff members will feel themselves to be corporately powerless, and will therefore exercise power only through individual deviance that will never see the light of day in supervision. In any case, staff development without increased power is non-sense.

## Social

Some things are almost inevitably achieved by the sheer fact of having staff meetings but it is rather more difficult to legislate for exactly *what* will be achieved. The social dimension of some staff meetings is to leave staff 'high', or feeling unwanted and unappreciated, or that they are not trusted; or to polarize attitudes; or to act as a means of contagion for all the negative feelings around in the staff group. Such feelings are not conducive to effective work together. Nor do they provide a good foundation for supervision.

Let us look, then, at some important aspects of the social side of the staff meeting, to which a Head of Home needs to attend.

(1) The ritual aspect: this is one of the things that tends to be achieved without anyone noticing it, apart from getting an uneasy feeling when for some reason it doesn't happen. When the members of a residential team sit down together to have a meeting, they are reminded that for better or for worse they *are* in fact members of the same team. They see that they have some responsibility to, and perhaps for, each other. This may not be articulated, but is there, and when there is a spate of sickness, or a batch of holidays, reducing the numbers of the group, this feeling becomes clearer. Similarly, in a working week characterized by the division of time into 'on-duty' and 'off-duty' periods, shifts, overtime, sleep-ins and change-overs, the staff meeting provides an element of essential continuity – a

reminder that the establishment goes on all the time. There are occasions when the ritual can swamp the task, but experience suggests that most of the time it is a comfortable undercurrent.

(2) Following on from ritual, there is the matter of representation; and a Head of Home does well to pay attention to this (see p. 15). It can be a source of great strength to an individual member of staff to feel that he does not work simply as an individual, but as a representative of a team. If he fails, someone else will come along and may succeed. (Bramham (1980) shows how the ideology of child care sets out to counter any corresponding feelings amongst residents.) He does not make demands or exercise authority purely on his own behalf, but on behalf of colleagues and the team as a whole. If the team never meets as a whole, however, it is far more difficult to feel this and to carry it through into practice.

There are dangers inherent in this feeling of corporateness. First, there is the possibility of it going overboard, to the point where individuality is forgotten and individual responsibility is abrogated with the notorious phrase, 'I was only obeying orders' (Milgram 1973). Second, the associated issue of how dissenting voices on unit policy are handled; whether conscience is railroaded by corporate commitment. And third, following from this, is the matter of whether staff feel themselves to be representatives of the whole staff team or of just one sub-group within it, and find themselves fighting for vested interests to the detriment of the whole. Within the staff meeting these issues translate into matters of trust, of inclusion and exclusion, and of the way in which opposition is handled.

Because supervision is individualized, it cannot handle such matters properly, although it may provide a forum for reflection on them. However, staff will take supervision seriously only if they feel some sense of being representatives of a team, and so the Head of Home also needs to attend to this dimension of staff meetings.

(3) In the introduction to this section on social aspects, I

painted a rather negative picture of 'some' staff meetings and how they left staff. The staff team that does not experience some conflict and tension, however happy and harmonious it may be on the whole, probably does not exist. If it does exist, it does so only because it is dead; tension is at the heart of life, and can and must be seen as a creative force. As with the other issues I have mentioned, its management is a matter of balance. So another part of the social management job of the Head of Home is to seek 'closure' on the meeting, and on individual items discussed in it. This does not mean the prohibition of further debate, but the creation of an atmosphere which contributes to ensuring that the discussion and disagreement have been cooled to manageable proportions by the time the meeting ends. If possible without the sacrifice of honesty and truth, people should leave the meeting feeling better and more at one with each other than they were when they came in. Only if such closure is satisfactorily achieved is it possible to conduct supervision without it being continually contaminated by unresolved business from the staff meeting (see also Chapter 6, 'The Supervision Session').

Staff meetings are not intended to be 'inspirational' events, like sales conventions in the United States. But both the fact that they happen and the way they are handled provide an important part of the foundation for a programme of supervision.

THE SUPERVISOR

The qualities of the supervisor have a chapter to themselves later on (Chapter 10), but in this section on ground-clearing I must mention her needs. Supervision is a process of support, among other things, and that entails the transfer of stress from one person to another. You can if you like see the supervisor as a buttress (even a flying buttress) on the outside of a cathedral. Because they are there on the outside to take some of the weight of the roof transmitted down on to the walls, it is possible to have the light soaring filigree of walls and window tracery that make for the airiness and beauty of Gothic and later cathedrals. Before their invention, all the weight had to be carried by the walls themselves, which consequently had to be very thick and rather clumsy, with little strength to spare for windows, contributing to the gloomy mystery of Norman and Romanesque churches. In the same way, open practice in residential work, with little reliance on survival tactics, depends in large part on the availability of the buttress to receive and accept some of the strain. But where does the pressure go to when the buttress has got it? The buttress itself needs a firm foundation, and perhaps another buttress to take the residual strain off *it*. Abandoning the analogy lest it be pushed too far (although it makes better sense to read the term 'key-worker' in architectural – 'key-stone worker' – than in 'lock' terms), it is still easy to see that if one is a senior member of staff in a residential establishment, one's job will be fairly stressful in itself. Now one is preparing to take on some of the strain of the rest of the staff as well. It is only reasonable to suppose that in order to do this effectively one will need one's own support system.

It is important to enter a qualification at this point. One is not in the business of relieving stress simply for the sake of it, but so that more of it can be tolerated by the staff. The staff will find ways of surviving, somehow. Those survival mechanisms may, however, include insensitivity to the needs of clients, unthinking authoritarianism, and short-term thinking – in other words, techniques that enable them to cope with stress at the cost of increasing it amongst the clients, who have enough stress in their lives already. The supervisor invites staff to pass on some of their feelings to him, so that they in turn can take on some more from the clients. There is nothing mystical or weird about this; it comes down to simple things like being more patient, thinking about the possible impact of a course of action before taking it, and if not being more tolerant (not always a desirable thing in itself) at least being consistent in what is tolerated and what is not.

So the problem often is that, if your own job gets any more

stressful, you may yourself become impatient, snappy, and inconsistent. This may be passed on to the residents and staff, in which case the situation is no better than before; or it may be passed on to your own family, which is being unfair and widening the circle of destruction instead of containing it. One fortunate feature of the communication of stress is that it becomes more diffuse as it gets further from the source, and this does provide the opportunity to make use of a further link in the chain to provide the final container. On the managerial side, the buck may be routed through senior staff to the Homes Adviser (or Residential Services Officer), to the Assistant Director, and to the Director of Social Services. On the professional/personal side, it will probably stop with the supervisor's supervisor. Who this is will depend in part on who is available among your network of contacts, and in part on personal needs.

The kind of supervisor who needs someone to pull her up, make her clarify her thinking, and ask awkward questions needs to choose someone whom she does not know too well, who can keep a clear professional distance, who will be available for a set period at set intervals, and who can be respected rather than liked. This person may not even be in residential work, but will have a clear and vigorous mind. The parallel is with the psychoanalyst's own analyst. His approach will not be sympathetic, but probing, forcing the supervisor to face up to the awkward questions that she fudges from day to day: the cold shower rather than warm bath approach.

On the other hand, the warm bath is equally important. The supervisor may be the kind of person who just gets 'up to *here*' with everything that's going on and the demands people are making on him, and needs someone to blurt it all out to, on demand. His supervisor will need to be someone rather closer, available on demand rather than at set times, sympathetic although not entirely uncritical, who can draw off all the pressure that makes his head feel as if it will burst, and who will leave him feeling that at least *someone* understands. This may be a spouse or close friend, or anyone except a colleague from the same establishment.

In practice, you will almost certainly feel the need for both kinds of support, and then the arguments have to be weighed for and against having separate people to deal with the two ends of the spectrum. It takes a lot of skill to handle both ends. On the one hand, if separate people are used for the cold shower and the warm bath, one may be set unconsciously against the other – in particular using the warm bath to justify ignoring the painful effects of the cold shower. In other words, either you have to contain in yourself the tension between the two different tasks (two people), or you have to find someone else who can do it (one person). If in doubt, err on the side of the cold shower, because the odds are that there is already a warm bath waiting somewhere.

A significant factor in successful supervision practice is the ability of the supervisor to make use of supervision himself. It is important to work with your own supervisor on how effectively you are using what he is offering, imperfect though it may be. It is equally important to get started *at once*, and for your supervisor to help in setting up the supervision programme in the establishment, because it is at its most frustrating and bewildering in the early stages.

None of the above should be taken as a substitute for training for supervision. The fact that the reader has got this far in this book is probably some indication of motivation and commitment, but books alone are not enough. There is no substitute for 'safe' practice – where mistakes do not have fearful consequences – such as can be gained through role-play and exercises on a good short course.

# 4 The Supervision Contract

The contract provides the framework for what happens in the supervision session and defines the task in specific terms. It is the first stage in the process of translating objectives into practice. Roles and behaviour in the supervision session follow from the contract, and this is why it is being discussed before, say, the qualities of the supervisor. However, many people find the idea of the contract difficult to work with, and shy away from it, so it needs a few words of explanation first.

*An explicit contract is a statement by both supervisor and staff member about the objectives and topics of their particular supervision sessions, and what each will do in order to meet these objectives.* This sounds simple enough, and perhaps it is the very simplicity of the idea that leads some people to believe that they can get by without making it explicit. One *can* get by without spelling it out, but only at the probable cost of a lot of misunderstanding and wasted time.

## WHY MAKE A CONTRACT?

Many people claim that an explicit contract is not necessary. They start off along the lines of 'We both know what we're here for, so let's get on with it. There's no need to muck about with all this stuff. . . . Besides, there are more urgent things to attend to. Now, about the holiday . . .' When supervision has been going on for a long time – months rather than weeks – it may be that there is sufficient understanding between both parties for the contract to drop into the background and become unspoken. But until that stage has been reached, it is the only way of making sure that both partners are talking about the same things and working towards the same objectives.

The alternative to an explicit contract is an implicit one, which evolves on an informal basis. Attractive as that idea sounds, it is fraught with problems. The first is that *supervisor and staff member many understand it differently*:

> 'I think we're meeting in order to improve my professional working skills, as part of my career development. You apparently think it is in order to get me to accept your way of doing things in this establishment and to stop me throwing unintentional spanners in the works.'

> 'I think I'm pretty good with the kids. You think that they clam up every time they see me and they are scared stiff of me.'

Such different orientations mean that the session is working at cross-purposes most of the time. Yet because the contract is not explicit there seems to be a conspiracy to avoid the basic differences, which may be more comfortable but often means the loss of learning opportunities.

The second problem with the informal contract is that *it is too changeable*. All contracts can be amended and developed in the light of changing circumstances and of learning, but the informal contract can be changed simply by the mood of the participants.

Suppose that you were on call last night, and you had to get up three times because of problems with a wandering resident. The last thing you feel like at the moment is an intense supervision session, so you either scrub it or you let it ride as a pleasant chat. I, the staff member, am full of something I want to get off my chest, but I find you discounting it and telling me to forget it. The contract seems to have changed, but no one has told me that it has. I feel frustrated and resolve that I'll keep things to myself in future.

The existence of a formal contract is not going to change feelings of exhaustion, but it does encourage the supervisor to explain:

'Look, I've been up most of the night, and I really can't do justice to the issues you are raising at the moment. If you are really bursting to talk about them now, then go ahead, but I'm not at my best and there is no way I can give you full value. If they're not that urgent, can we leave them until next time?'

The staff member may be disappointed, but now she does have a realistic choice to make, one she can work with. Informal contracts are contracts for flight; if the participants do not tie down what the session is about, then it is all too easy to drift off into gossip about work in general. Gossip may have its uses and its place, but it is not the same thing as supervision. If the contract is not explicit neither participant can appeal to it as a means of hauling the discussion back on to the right lines.

The third problem with the inarticulate contract is that, if a contract is not clear to both participants, *it cannot provide a boundary or container to what happens in the session.* There are occasions in serious 'normal' conversation when people make remarks of the order of 'Do you mind if I speak frankly?' or 'Stop beating about the bush – spit it out!' These are requests or demands for a temporary contract to go beyond the normal limitations of polite conversation. If one person is then offended, the other can legitimately say, 'Well, you asked for it – literally', and need not feel guilt at having overstepped the bounds of propriety. In this case, the contract (however temporary) acts as a container for the feelings involved and prevents them from getting out of hand or contaminating the rest of the relationship. The supervision contract helps to establish the special conditions that apply within the supervision session and nowhere else. But unless it is explicit, it cannot do this.

In short, the contract constitutes the 'rules of the game'. You would be unlikely to enter into, say, a game of cards without knowing clearly what the rules were in advance. You would certainly object if the rules were changed in the middle of play.

## DIFFICULTIES WITH FORMAL CONTRACTS

Acknowledging that a contract is needed is still not really enough to get over the hurdle of embarrassment when it comes to drafting one, face to face with a staff member. It feels like taking steps away from each other. It feels as though, by putting the talk on a formal basis, one is calling into question years of working together, in particular the unspoken understanding of the other's attitudes and values. These feelings are often strong enough to lead a supervisor to fudge the issue. It is better to share the feeling:

> 'You know, doing this makes me feel as if we're drawing up a legal document, as if we don't trust each other. It's not like that, but supervision is different from the usual chats we've been having up to now, and I think it's important we should get it right from the beginning. So . . .'

There may also be a feeling that it is all really a bit of an affectation: 'Here we are, making such a big deal out of something that is really quite straightforward.'

This is indeed a problem, because the trappings of supervision, including the contract, do not of themselves make it work. I go along with anyone who would rather understate than overstate things. But the problem of affectation rears its head only if importance is attached to it; in other words, it is a self-fulfilling prophecy. (On the power of self-fulfilling prophecies in social work see Smail 1982.) The best way out of it is paradoxically to devote time to the contract. Spend several sessions on it, as a routine first step in supervision. Go through the job description in one or two sessions, and then move on to specific talents and areas of weakness for another one or two. The process will, by then, feel relatively comfortable. What is more, that kind of structure reduces anxiety in the first few sessions.

Before leaving the reasons for and difficulties of the contract, there is a sting in the tail. I have looked at the 'honourable' reasons for wondering whether a contract is worth while; but there is also a 'dishonourable' one, which is powerful and quite common. This is the hidden desire, which may not be apparent to either party, to have supervision fail – or, in its minor form, to build in a device to ensure that one cannot tell whether it is succeeding or failing. This has to be mentioned, because it comes up again and again in all areas of social work. A fieldworker refuses or neglects to spell out in detail what she is aiming at in a particular case, because then she can't be blamed for not achieving it. This stems from a fantasy of omnipotence, as if it were up to her alone whether the client's circumstances changed or not. A 'treatment plan' in residential care is couched in such vague terms that no one can tell whether it has worked or not. Supervision programmes are left aimless so that either they are bound to collapse, or they can never be properly assessed. What lies behind all this fudging and vagueness is the fear of failure, particularly the social worker's primary fear of being found to be useless.

However committed both supervisor and staff are to the idea of supervision, and however much they tell each other so, there is *always* this residual reluctance and resistance, even if it is unconscious. Making the programme fail, either by ignoring the contract or in another way, is a good (or rather 'effective') way of getting out of doing supervision, because it appears to have been tried and found not to work. One cannot deal with this game in any other way than by confronting it – which requires that one acknowledge at least the possibility that one plays it. (See Kadushin 1976 for other games that may be played in supervision.)

## BASIC CONTRACT PROVISIONS

Although the essence of the contract is that in detail it is different for each supervision pair, the basic shape of most contracts can be described fairly easily. It will be in two parts: the first common to all staff, referred to here as the 'basic provisions'; the second tailored for each individual staff member, referred to as 'specific provisions'. The basic provisions cover the arrangements for the meetings and the common framework of the programme. The specific provisions are dealt with in the next chapter.

First of all, the basic provisions need to include *agreements about the boundaries of the sessions*. Such agreements will specify time and place, duration and frequency of meetings, people to be present, and so on. This is obvious, but the formal statement of such factors has implications that are worth examining. If arrangements are spelt out in such a way that there is no possibility of misunderstanding them, you can be pretty sure that either the meeting will take place or some good reason can be found for it not happening. Sometimes such a good reason will take the form of something really unexpected and important cropping up in the establishment, which does require the attention of one person or another at short notice. Sometimes the 'good reason' is something that was obviously avoidable, in which case it is reasonable to suppose that there is some overt or covert resistance to coming to the session. If one member just forgets, that says something as well. But if the arrangements have been left casual and uncertain (as in 'informal' supervision), there are so many loopholes and 'get-outs' in the obscurity of date, time, and place that there is no basis for challenging someone for not having kept to them. This is far from a matter of trying to catch a staff member out; it is a question of making boundaries clear so that reasonable conclusions can be drawn from the way they are negotiated. As an experienced practitioner commented on the use of contracts in social work in general: 'The interesting thing about contracts is not what happens when they are kept, but what happens when they are broken.'

If tight arrangements give a chance to test the commitment of the staff member, they also test the dependability of the supervisor. If you make a casual arrangement with a social acquaintance, such as 'Do come round some time', the imprecision of the invitation indicates that it is not meant to be taken particularly seriously. If, on the other hand, you go on to specify a date and time, then it is a much more powerful arrangement. The preparedness of a supervisor to commit part of his busy diary, some way ahead, and to indicate that his commitment will not be changed by other claims on his time – this gives an indication of the importance he attaches to supervision; whether he meets that commitment gives an idea of his dependability.

Many supervisors are reluctant to make definite forward commitments of this kind: 'You can never tell what's going to happen next in residential work. I can't commit myself that far in advance.' In order to be realistic, and granting that supervision is not, and ought not to be, the most important part of the job, it is worth considering under what circumstances you might feel obliged to change arrangements already made. What would take priority over a supervision session? Court appearances? Almost certainly. Reviews? Probably. A promise to a resident to take her to the dentist, personally? Perhaps. If you know what your priorities are, then you can at least be straight with your partner. But if everything else comes before supervision, as it often seems to, then that indicates how little importance is attached to it.

## Openness vs confidentiality

A similar kind of exercise of clarification of priorities applies to contract provisions affecting confidentiality. This is an awkward issue in supervision as in other areas of social work, where the general rule seems to be blithely to give assurances of confidentiality and then to get into terrible messes about them afterwards.

Confidentiality is not the same thing as secrecy. Secrecy means that you will not divulge information to anyone else under any circumstances; confidentiality, in practice, means that the circumstances in which information will be divulged are understood by both parties and consented to. Confidentiality is about confidence and confidences, and that is why it matters in supervision. There is a case for saying that everything talked about should have the status of public knowledge unless there is good reason for it to be otherwise – in other words, to put the onus on establishing the need for confidentiality, rather than on exceptions to a rule of secrecy. Why, then, might some form of confidentiality be useful in supervision?

First, staff members are more likely to be forthcoming about their problems and difficulties in their work if they have some assurance that the supervisor is not going to talk about them to all and sundry. Second, the 'information-control' aspect of confidentiality provides a convenient test for other aspects of confidence. I (staff member) may not be sure about your (supervisor's) abilities in the initial stages of supervision, but until your competence can be demonstrated in other ways, at least your ability to respect a confidence allows me to feel that I am not ruining my career by opening up to you in our sessions. In practice, I may well put you through the hoops – test you out – in respect of confidentiality in the early stages of supervision.

Establishing the guidelines of confidentiality in the supervision contract therefore has its complexities. The staff member is likely to want them to be relatively rigid, approximating to secrecy. The supervisor is likely to want them more flexible, bearing in mind her management responsibilities. Setting out the limits is difficult in the abstract, because the culture of the establishment will also affect them, but the provisions in the specimen contracts (*Figures 3 and 4*, pp. 58–61) give guidelines starting from either the secrecy or the openness ends.

This approach is not foolproof, and you can probably already think of situations in which it might be severely tested. But to make the limits any tighter is to become very legalistic, and to open the way to manipulative games. At least they give the staff member the option to keep quiet about material that the supervisor would have to pass on. This sounds like a negative argument, but from the point of view of the supervisor even this limited disclosure of information may tell her more about what is going on in the unit than she would have learnt without a supervision programme.

What about the staff member's side of the bargain? Generally speaking, the staff member does not give any such undertaking, and can talk about his supervision experience as much as he likes. This follows from the notion that the need for confidentiality has to be established before it is brought into play. In supervision, the staff member is in the more vulnerable position, and therefore confidentiality provisions protect him; the supervisor is not seen as having the same need. This gives the staff member a certain amount of power that the supervisor does not have. He can, if he wishes, go around telling all kinds of stories about his supervision and his supervisor without her having the right of reply. It may be important for the staff member to have this kind of power over the supervisor, which she has to learn to live with.

An important practice point arises from this (and may well be discussed when the confidentiality provision is being negotiated). What is the extent of the confidentiality provision in the implicit contract with clients? Can they, and ought they to be able to, say things to staff that will not be passed on (even in supervision)? If not, why are their rights different from those of staff?

Before we leave the matter of confidentiality, it is worth looking at two special cases. The first concerns the right of the supervisor to use material in her own supervision sessions. If she is to get beyond generalities in her work with her own supervisor, she has to talk about her work in a direct way, and that probably means getting clearance from her supervisees to do so.

The second case concerns what happens when one staff member complains about another in a supervision session. (See also the section on staff roles, p. 99 ff.) This really puts the confidentiality/collusion issue on the line, especially if the same supervisor is working with both the staff members concerned. There is no perfect solution to this problem – which is in any case familiar to anyone in residential work, because it is always coming up in disputes between residents. The following guidelines may help:

– The first is not to take the situation purely at its face value, but to look behind it. Why is the issue being brought up in supervision, when there is the least opportunity to do anything constructive about it? Why is it not being raised in a staff meeting, or with a senior member of staff outside supervision? In other words, what game is being played? Another question: does the 'third-party' staff member know about the complaint? If not, why not? Issues of justice as well as of staff development enter at this point. This may come under the heading of professional ethics, and make the supervisor duty-bound to raise the matter with the third party.

– The second guideline comes into play at this point. The fact that a senior staff member is acting in the supervisor role does not mean that she has abandoned all managerial authority. Her authority and responsibility are to see that the clients are cared for; if staff rivalries interfere with that, then she is free to knock heads together, bawl people out, or do whatever she usually does. But it must be done in the open, using information that is public knowledge.

# 5 The Personalized Part of the Contract

While the basic provisions of the contract are usually proposed by the supervisor and then negotiated with the staff, the personalized part of the contract is often initiated the other way round. The supervisor invites the staff member to say what she wants to get out of the sessions; she puts some ideas forward, and then both work together to establish what can and cannot be done. The supervisor will have his own ideas about the areas the staff member needs to develop (and may indeed think that her ideas go in the wrong direction), but it is best to start with her own views. This is first because of the general rule of starting where the staff member is (or thinks she is), rather than where the supervisor thinks she ought to be, and second because resistance to supervision is reduced if staff feel that they can make some of the running, and that the pay-off is direct, definite, and recognizably to do with their own understanding of their needs.

It is now about the third supervision session. Both will probably be feeling that the job description has now been dealt with. So the supervisor says something like: 'OK – we seem to have done as much as we can on this. Now let's start to apply it. What do you want to work on in these sessions?' Sometimes the staff member will take her cue from an issue identified in the job description: 'Well, it's obvious I'm not too hot on the report-writing side of things.' The supervisor's reaction may well be that this is the least of her troubles, but even so he should not discount her perception, and should do something about it as he goes along. But he should not let it stop there: 'What else?'

CLARIFYING IDEAS

This is where the potential problems arise, in three forms:

(1) The staff member is hooked on the job description, and cannot see beyond it, so needs to be coaxed back to her direct experience of working with the clients.
(2) The staff member does not (or, it appears, *will* not) come up with the most important issues, which are glaringly obvious to the supervisor. The temptation is to overrule her, and bring down on her head a stunning catalogue of her failures and inadequacies as you see them. This is a recipe for disaster. She has to feel that she owns the supervision as much as the supervisor does, if not more so, and so at this stage it is important to let her make the running, even if she appears to be off the track.
(3) The staff member is too vague. This is the commonest problem, and requires more detailed examination.

Vague statements include: 'I want to improve my confidence', and 'I want to improve my relationships with the residents' (and even the devastating 'Don't know, really', to which we shall return later). One may be tempted to let such statements pass, as if it would be rude (or naïve) to enquire exactly what they mean. But do they give enough to go on? What is meant by 'confidence'? When does she feel least confident? When is she most confident? What sort of 'relationship'? What does she think her relationship with the residents ought to be like?

Jumping in immediately with 'What do you mean, "I want to improve my confidence"?' is likely to be heard as dismissive of a strong if woolly feeling. Be careful at this stage. Accept the point. Make a note of it. Then try to pin it down, gently. Ask for examples of times when the staff member has lacked confidence. Reflect back to her what she seems to be saying, and work on tightening up the ideas and the circumstances. After a while the suggestion will clarify and resolve itself into something like:

'Clients seem unwilling to approach me for anything except

to ask me for things. I want to know why that is, and to make myself more approachable.'

Or:

'I don't seem to be able to tell as well as the other staff when there is something brewing among the residents. I want to improve my skills in observation.'

There may be problems in these versions, but they are much more workable. What one is looking for is either a clear statement about where the staff member is now (as she understands it), expressed in fairly concrete terms, or a statement of where she wants to be, expressed in clear enough terms for both to recognize when she has reached that point.

## HARD AND SOFT CONTRACTS

The basic distinction is between objectives, and hence contract provisions, that are 'soft' and those that are 'hard'. Soft objectives and contracts cover a lot of ground, are rather generalized and woolly, and are characterized by the fact that it would be difficult for the supervisor (and sometimes for the staff member herself) to tell when they have been achieved. Hard objectives are much more limited in scope, are specific and to the point, and it is fairly easy to tell when they have been achieved. The general rule is: whenever possible make the objective and the contract *harder*. Tie them down to specific aspects of work and behaviour. If in doubt about their hardness, ask, 'What would count as evidence of this objective being achieved?' If you cannot think of anything, then the objective is far too soft and too broad, and perhaps too long-term. If you can conceive of some evidence, then why not make the achievement of that bit of behaviour itself into the objective?

Some examples:

'I want to be able to communicate better with adolescents' (*soft*).

'I want to be able to hold a conversation with Sharon and Debby for five minutes without them walking away or telling me to "piss off" (and without it costing me two cigarettes)' (*hard*).

'I want to be able to work better with Joan' (another member of staff) (*soft*).

'I want to be able to tell Joan how much it annoys me when she is so bossy and patronizing when we are bathing the residents' (*hard*).

'I want to be able to do some things my way when Joan and I are working together' (*hard*).

Because hard contracts are at a low level of abstraction, many of them are needed to cover the same ground as a soft one; this is shown in the third example above, where 'working better with Joan' has at least two elements, and probably many more. But hard contracts have an additional advantage, in that they provide a check on personal judgements about work, which often contain elements of fantasy. Thus the staff member may believe that he cannot communicate effectively with adolescents largely because Sharon and Debbie tell him to 'piss off' with monotonous regularity. His supervisor may well be able to reassure him that they react in exactly the same way to everyone, and that he is doing himself an injustice by generalizing from this particularly difficult case. Note, too, that the 'Joan' example also raises questions about the staff member's judgement of a colleague.

Most supervisors are too soft in defining the specific elements of the contract. The process of finding hard contract items to replace soft ones does not mean that the soft items (which may be much broader) should be forgotten. Instead, one may use a number of hard items to cover as much as possible of the area of the soft contract, bearing in mind that not all of it will be amenable to expression in hard terms (see *Figure 2*). Otherwise the soft contract (like 'I want to be more confident') can become so grandiose that both supervisor and staff member are overwhelmed by it. This process of

*Figure 2* Hard and soft contract elements

If a soft element looks like this, consider how it can be dealt with in harder terms:

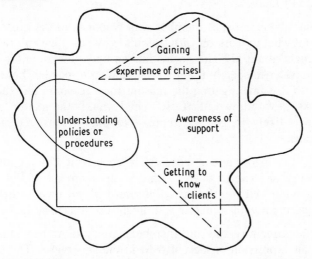

The hard elements do not cover all the ground of the soft one, but they do cover a lot of it. Solid lines show elements most appropriate to supervision; broken lines require outside work.

subdividing previously enormous soft goals into manageable, 'bite-sized' chunks is not simply a preparation for learning, it is a learning step in itself. In the course of acquiring the 'mini-skills' that go to make up the whole, the staff member may well find that he has acquired the key skill, after learning which everything else slots into place.

Just one qualification needs to be entered on the general principle of making objectives and contracts as hard as possible. This is the possibility that a supervisor can use the very hard contract as a means of controlling staff. The contract is so formulated that everything is seen as a set of precise skills to be learnt by staff, so that wider issues of establishment policy and the like can be ignored in supervision. Ultimately, this leads to an 'ours not to reason why' approach, which is sometimes found in the armed forces and in nursing training. This is inimical to the spirit of professional development that prompts the introduction of supervision in the first place.

### 'I don't know'

What about the staff member who responds to the question about what to work on with 'I don't know' or 'I haven't really thought about it'? This seems like an open invitation for the supervisor to specify the material, and so it may be, but it is worth first investigating the reasons for a response like this.

Ask a withdrawn, distressed child what is the matter, and one is likely to get the reply, 'Nothing.' Translated, that means,

'Quite a lot, and it goes fairly deep, but I don't know whether I can trust you with it at the moment, so I'm not going to tell you, because I'm safer with my own hurt than sharing it with someone who might use it against me.'

In the same way, the staff member's 'don't know' can equally be an expression of lack of trust in the supervisor. The task then of the supervisor is to work out a contract with the distrustful staff member that is both sufficiently non-threatening to provide material to work on and sufficiently real for the supervisor to use to demonstrate her trustworthiness. Remember, supervision is going to go on for a long time – for as long as you both work in the establishment – so there is no hurry.

The 'don't know' reply may be true. It can mean, 'There are so many things we could talk about. I've no idea where to start'; or it can mean, 'I've never done this kind of thing before. What is acceptable?' This is straightforward to deal with, because the staff member will grasp at any straw, and the conversation will probably go off like a rocket as soon as one mentions a particular resident, or an incident, or a procedure. This is often rather seductive, and although I do not want to discount the useful work that can be done in this way, I am convinced that it is not as useful as what can be achieved by formulating a contract.

'Don't know' can mean, 'You tell me.' And the supervisor often does. It is a device for avoiding the responsibility that comes from a joint ownership of the supervision programme. Whatever the work done, the basic foundation remains the fact of the supervisor doing it *to* the staff member. So the golden rule is not to fall for this one.

'Don't know' can also mean, 'Everything seems to be running relatively smoothly, so what is there to worry about?' It is in working at this attitude that supervision has so much to offer. Residential care can be carried out at a number of levels and can seem to operate satisfactorily at any of them (Atherton 1984b). Indeed, for anyone who is immersed in working at a given level, it is often difficult to imagine what would be involved in working in any other way. Professional supervision is a means of *raising the game* – of giving such workers a glimpse of what the higher levels look like. When someone cannot think of anything to talk about, he is effectively saying that he cannot visualize those higher levels or see how his work could be any different.

With this latter group of 'don't knows', too, the first step is learning to identify the issues *they* want to work on, even if they are not the same as those the supervisor would like to propose. But this does not mean that the supervisor has no right to suggest material for the contract. After all, she can provide an outsider's view of the staff member's practice, and this perspective is as important as that of the staff member himself. With the help of her own supervisor, she should seek to develop a climate in which the *differences* of the staff are valued as much as their similarities.


A CONTRACT FOR LEARNING

So the supervisor also adds his contribution to the contract suggestions. But he has to do it in such a way that he identifies the learning potential in each area he comments on. As a manager, he might be inclined to say:

> 'It's all very well taking time to talk to one or two of the old people, but you forget that just leaves one staff member for the other forty. You have to spread yourself around better.'

Or:

> 'I've noticed that you sometimes set up activities that get out of control. You've got to stop that. If you can't carry something through, don't start it.'

And in that capacity he is perfectly entitled to say it. As a supervisor, however, he has to look beyond the immediate problem, and ask himself how he can raise the issue in such a way as to give the staff member room to learn from it. He might therefore say:

> 'You've had quite a lot to do with Miss Slater, haven't you? I know she's a mine of fascinating stories – ex-missionary and all that – but you do tend to leave other people to do the routine work while you are chatting to her. Is there any way you can work out when you can afford time for that kind of chat, do you think? Have you any ideas as to how we can provide this kind of contact for all the residents?'

Or:

> 'I've noticed on a couple of occasions recently that you have

set up an activity that has got rather out of control. There are a whole lot of reasons why that might happen, of course; I thought we might look at them together and see what we might learn from the experience – and possibly plan your next activity together, allowing for that kind of thing.'

Note that in these cases, the supervisor refers to specific instances. He does not tell the staff member off for laziness, or imply that the activity has been a complete shambles from beginning to end. In the second case he indicates that there are many possible reasons why things went wrong (not all of them coming down to the sheer incompetence of the staff member), and emphasizes a shared investigation of the situation and planning for next time. The staff member – acutely and embarrassedly aware of the fiascos behind her – may well mis-hear all this, but if the supervisor had not said it right in the first place there would be no chance of being heard properly. The supervisor has to put items on the agenda in such a way that they fit with the spirit and overall aims and values of supervision.

He may also wish to raise points for the contract about particular relationships between clients and the staff member:

'It seems to me that Stanley is able to manipulate you – and you don't see it coming or when you are setting yourself up for it. [Specific examples quoted.] I think we ought to keep an eye on this, so that we can discuss incidents as they come up and find a way of handling them.'

'I've noticed that, much as she tries to cover it up, Sandra does seem to listen when you are talking – like the other night at tea, when . . . It's possible that someone has got through to her at last! Let's put that on our agenda so that know what we are hoping to achieve through this relationship if and when it does develop.'

The first example is the more delicate one, because it is and must be critical. Staff members should be able to take being criticized, certainly, but they need to receive the message in such a way that they acknowledge the legitimacy of the point being made, and do not get defensive. After all, being defensive is simply a waste of energy that could be spent in learning. But the second example is just as important, because it involves planning ahead and also helping a staff member to recognize a new responsibility.

REACHING AN AGREEMENT

Everything so far about personalized contract material has been about putting ideas forward, and the emphasis has been on those items that make demands on the staff member. It remains, therefore, to point out that *a contract is a contract only when it is mutually agreed*, and that it involves obligations for both sides. The fact that an item is suggested as part of the initial contract does not mean that the other side has to accept it.

I am usually pleased when some suggestions are not accepted. If I make a fairly intense point, and my supervisee responds by saying, 'Yes, I think that is an issue, and we'll have to get into it some time, but I'm not ready for it yet', that is fine by me, because it sounds like a very reasonable judgement. It means that the supervisee is not just agreeing for the sake of it, and augurs well for the items we do agree on. (Sometimes, of course, I am wrong.) If, on the other hand, a point is accepted grudgingly, 'Well . . . yes . . . I suppose so', then I wonder whether we have a realistic contract. However, if I do get an agreement, albeit a grudging and half-hearted one, I let it stand for the moment. If the supervisee backs off from it later, I then refer back to the original contract, emphasizing that I took her agreement at face value. On a few occasions this has led to us renegotiating the whole contract much more realistically. (Readers familiar with Transactional Analysis, which also relies heavily on contracts in therapy, will recognize that the above is a description of an Adult–Adult agreement, rather than a Parent–Adapted Child one; see Berne 1961 and 1966a, in particular.)

The whole process of drawing up the contract is much more convincing and focused if it is written up and both parties have a copy. The supervisee can be responsible for this. Items do not have to be ticked off at each session, but it helps to have the contract there as a concrete record of what was agreed at the beginning of the programme. (See Chapter 7, 'Recording and Monitoring'.)

## BENEFITS FOR THE SUPERVISEE

What does the supervisee get out of this? So far, all the supervisor has agreed to do is to give some time to the supervision session. The staff member is entitled to ask for more specific things from supervision. She may ask for feedback on her performance in certain situations. She may ask for her reports to be read and commented on. She may ask for some managerial assistance – such as changing the shift team with whom she works, or getting experience in another unit. In any case, the undertakings given by the supervisor are just as binding as those that the supervisee gives, and they therefore need to be as carefully considered. The staff member has only one supervision programme to deal with, and thus only one set of contract obligations; the supervisor on the other hand may have five or six to handle, and if he over-commits himself to work on one of them the others will lose out. So although he will rightly be concerned to give each staff member good value, he should not be afraid to set out the limits of what can realistically be offered; it is much better to do this in the opening stages than to let someone down later on.

## WORKING WITH THE CONTRACT

We have spent so long discussing the contract that by now it may seem to be an enormous document, and one problem that crops up now and again is that a contract becomes so unwieldy as to be useless. Remember that the average length of time available for any one item in any one session is the length of the session divided by the number of items. There may be some routine 'check' items, and not everything on the list will be discussed at every meeting; but even so, there should be no more than five or six items 'live' at any one time, and you should not reckon on working on more than two or perhaps three of them in any one session. Just as supervision as a whole cannot be hurried, so any part of it needs enough time to develop and be explored. Broadly speaking, it takes about three-quarters of an hour to introduce new work, twenty minutes to pick up the threads of ongoing work and to add something useful to it. If you are working very much faster than this, then you need to ask whether this is really giving the staff member enough time to open up, or whether he is being steamrollered.

Contracts should not be strait-jackets. Paradoxically perhaps, in view of everything I have said about them up to now, they ought hardly to be noticeable once you get going. They should fit like comfortable old shoes, providing support and structure, enabling you to reach places you would not otherwise be able to go into, but barely noticeable in wear. You have to be flexible; if a staff member has just got caught up in a crisis, it is daft to say that it cannot be discussed in supervision because it is not in the contract, and it will have to wait its turn. But if it appears that more often than not you are leaving the contract to deal with immediate issues, or with other things that seem more live at the time, then the contract does not pass the test of keeping in touch with reality. This happens fairly frequently, and it is one of the factors that have got contracts a bad name. For this reason some supervisors like to delay the formulation of the contract until major themes have emerged naturally from the supervision. There is something to be said for this approach, which is really one of monitoring the implicit contract and eventually making it explicit, but it is a variation that on the whole I would commend mainly to more experienced practitioners.

CHANGING THE CONTRACT

There is nothing wrong with changing the contract. Indeed, it is essential to keep it under constant review in the background, because it is meant to be a *reflection* of the supervision task, rather than to dominate it. There is therefore no need to make a big deal out of changing it, or to set time aside for contract reviews in a special session. Just use it as a summing-up device:

> 'Well, in this session we've had a go at the incident at the fair, and then we got on to Jerry and his home visits. I think that needs a continuing watch, so let's put it into the contract to remind me, shall we? Now, this business I raised at the beginning about counselling . . . we haven't really touched it at all in the last couple of months. I still think it is important, but let's put it on one side for the moment. Is that OK with you? Is there anything else we ought to include to remind ourselves to look at next session?'

The casualness of this kind of review does not absolve the supervisor from the responsibility of making a proper contract about Jerry's home visits and the worker's role in relation to them; a list of topics is not a contract. But doing it this way reinforces the idea of the contract as servant rather than master.

Sometimes the turnover of contract items may be quite fast. This may well be accounted for by the rate of change in the establishment at large. Equally, the contract may sometimes remain substantially unchanged for months on end. There is no general rule about how long any item should remain on the books, but it is a useful discipline for supervisors to reflect on the turnover rate together with their own supervisor. If it is very fast, with items being taken up for one or perhaps two sessions and then dropped again, this could suggest several things. It could mean that the topics chosen are too precise, too 'hard', and perhaps too trivial; the sessions may simply be dealing in hints and tips and not moving on to the principles involved, which is what supervision is all about. Or high turnover may indicate that the supervisor is not seeing the connections and resemblances between the items being raised; in which case she is reinforcing the worker's tendency to treat every situation and every client as discrete and isolated from every other. Or it may suggest that the staff member is shadow-boxing – raising a succession of trivial items either to

*Figure 3* Specimen contract 1

| Contract | Notes |
|---|---|

Supervision contract between D.S. (RSW Grade 2) (supervisee) and J.F. (Deputy Head of Home) (supervisor)

*Basic provisions*

(1) The supervision programme is designed
   (a) to ensure continuing support,
   (b) provide an individualized programme of development,
   for each staff member.

This contract has all the hallmarks of having been hammered out in staff meeting and other discussions; it is stilted and pseudo-legal in style. But if that is the price of an extensive process of consultation that results in general consensus, it is well worth it.

(2) Each staff member will be supervised by someone senior to him/her in the establishment. In the event of anyone not being able to establish a suitable working relationship, the decision about changing the pair will rest with the Head of Home.

Note that *either partner* can request a change, and the procedure is laid down. But it is left to common sense what is a 'suitable working relationship'.

(3) Supervision sessions will take place at least once every three weeks for 45 minutes, at a time acceptable to both partners. Date, time, and place of the next *two* meetings will be arranged/confirmed at each session.

The commitment is clear, but note that the provisions relate only to the minimum time the staff member is entitled to.

(4) Supervision commitments will take priority over everything except:
   (a) staffing emergencies that would leave only one person on duty when children are at home (e.g. during school holidays);
   (b) court appearances;
   (c) case conferences directly involving either partner.

One may feel that this kind of precision is tempting providence! It may not work, but if it works well enough to be taken seriously, it demonstrates the importance given to supervision.

(5) The content of supervision will be open for discussion by either member with colleagues within the establishment

This contract starts from the 'open' end; the onus is on the person who wants it to be confidential to say

(6) The record of supervision will be the responsibility of the supervisee, who will keep it and make it available to the supervisor as needed. The supervisee also has the right to see any informal notes kept by the supervisor, which will be destroyed after the session following that to which they relate.

This follows the pattern suggested in this book; but note the extra provision to ensure that there is no unaccountable 'underground' record existing after it has served its immediate purpose.

*Specific provisions*

(7) D.S. will use supervision to monitor the progress of his key clients.

This is the kind of item that will remain in the contract for all time, but may need to be amended by more specific items relating to particular residents from time to time.

(8) D.S. wants to know more about therapeutic approaches in work with adolescents, and J.F. agrees to keep him supplied with articles on this and to discuss them.

This is a frequent kind of 'early' item: perhaps a little too academic for supervision, but accepted by the supervisor as a token of starting where the supervisee want to start. Note the undertaking given by the supervisor, which must be carried out.

(9) D.S. agrees to discuss occasions when he loses his temper with clients and to see what causes it and how he can control it. J.F. will watch for such situations when they are working together.

This is much harder and more personal. The phrasing suggest that the idea came from the supervisor in the first place.

(10) J.F. would like D.S. to look at his priorities, especially in terms of the effect on the young people of his programme of sporting activities. D.S. agrees, as the situation arises.

This is a sort of stand-by clause, in that it will not be discussed regularly; but it indicates that both partners are aware of the issue and are prepared to look at it when it becomes a problem.

Signed . . . . . . . . . . . . . . . . (D.S.)    . . . . . . . . . . . . . . . . (J.F.)    Date . . . . . . . . . . . . . .

*Figure 4* Specimen contract 2

## Contract

Kathleen Adams and Maureen Beasley, supervised by Ann Thompson (3rd officer)

*We agree that:*

(1) Supervision is a regular meeting to help staff to do their jobs as well as possible.

(2) We shall meet monthly and fix the date at least one week in advance; this is Ann's job, since she has access to the rotas. Normally we shall meet for half an hour after the afternoon drinks trolley has been round. If either Kathleen or Maureen cannot make it, we shall go ahead, but Ann will see the absent member as soon as possible afterwards.

(3) We shall keep supervision sessions confidential except where they deal with material suitable for the staff meeting, or where all of us agree not to.

(4) Each of us in turn will make brief notes of the meeting, and the folder of notes will be kept by that person until the next session.

(5) We may include other people in our discussions if we all agree to do so.

## Notes

This contract relates to the supervision of two care assistants in an old people's home, and is far less formal than the first example, being basically a set of notes drawn up between the three of them, but meaning the same thing as the more 'legalistic' document.

Very simple, but adequate.

A realistic compromise with the pressures of time and uncertainty in planning ahead.

A bit loose, this part; it accepts non-attendance too readily, and thus implicitly does not give supervision much value.

Presumably the choice of the confidentiality option says something about the uncertainty of the participants. It does not seem consistent with the style of the rest of the contract, which is informal, or the items listed for discussion.

Another simple system, although the concentration on the contents of the discussion limits its use as a monitoring device.

Useful provision; but how does it fit with item (3)?

(6) We shall discuss the routine procedures in the Home to make sure that Kathleen and Maureen understand the reasons for them.

There are some definite implications here for work outside the sessions.

(7) Each time we meet we will agree to observe particular residents so that in the next session we can talk about their needs and how we meet them.

Good idea in principle, helpful to all three participants, but is it practicable in half an hour a month?

(8) Ann will pass on any interesting material she is getting from her in-service course.

Again, the infrequency of meeting limits the effectiveness of a good idea.

(9) We agree to raise any problems we have in working with each other, if possible before involving anyone else.

Clearly a necessary addition; it looks as if the sessions were getting swamped with inappropriate material.

((9a) We agree to *exclude* anything to do with the planning for the Summer Fayre, with which we are all involved.)

(10) We can change this contract at any time if we all agree.

Signed ..................................

..................................

..................................

Date ..................................

test out the supervisor or to defend against something more important and/or painful being talked about.

If issues never seem to disappear from the contract, and nothing is ever added, that also suggests some possibilities. It could mean that the contract items are too soft – in the sense either that you can never tell when you are making progress with them, or of having delusions of psychotherapy. It could mean that, irrespective of the contract provisions, supervision is caught up in some game, perhaps of over-intellectualizing, which has pay-offs for both parties but may not effectively serve the task. Or it may suggest that the contract was forgotten long ago.

CONCLUSION

The supervision contract is a way of clarifying what supervision is about, in order that staff member and supervisor together know what they need to put into it, and what they are hoping to get out of it. An important spin-off is that it provides a device to monitor where supervision is going. Since it is of the essence of the contract that it is shared and agreed by both parties, it makes sense for it to be written down and for both to have copies of it.

The two 'specimen contracts' – *Figures 3* and *4* – are each designed to illustrate some features of the foregoing discussion. Seeing a contract in isolation in a book gives a very poor guide to its worth or effectiveness, but the reader may find it worth while to examine these specimens, perhaps with colleagues, and to evaluate them. Each specimen is accompanied by a column of 'Notes', raising some of the issues that occur to me about them. Neither the specimens themselves nor the notes are intended to be perfect or to be taken as models, but rather as discussion-starters.

It is a mistake to see the contract as an end in itself. It is simply part of the framework of the building. The part of supervision that makes the difference has yet to come, where the outline or framework is filled in. But without the framework, you may well be filling in the wrong bits.

# 6 The Supervision Session

It is now time to consider the conduct of the supervision session itself. It is clear that the session needs to have some kind of structure to it, and that this is largely provided by the contract, but there is also the matter of pacing it so as to make the most effective use of the time available. A balance has to be struck between too little structure, which leads to a rambling and inconclusive session (but may also permit new insights and creativity that would not be found if it were too controlled), and too much structure, which makes the whole thing into a ritual dance.

There are three basic parts to the supervision session. These are, not surprisingly, the beginning, the middle, and the end.

## The beginning

There are two jobs to be done at the beginning of the session, although they are often done so naturally and quickly that one is not aware of them at all. Nevertheless, if they are not done, they will affect all the rest of the session, and possibly subsequent sessions as well.

The first of these is at the *maintenance level*; that is to say, it is concerned with setting up the right kind of relationship between the supervisor and the staff member. The physical setting can be important to conveying messages about this. Very often there is no perfect place to have supervision that can be guaranteed to be free of all interruptions, but it is useful to be able to use the same place for every session, and to lay it out as well as possible for the purpose of supervision. In many residential establishments, the sleeping-in room is a convenient choice (although it has the disadvantage of having a telephone). In day-care establishments, one has to improvise. In any case, the room needs to carry connotations of work, but should preferably not be the main office – both because of interruptions and because of its assocation with management. Provide two chairs that are equally comfortable, and if possible a table between them with some large sheets of paper and felt-tip pens. If all this is laid out beforehand (or if both of you go to the trouble of setting it up together), the setting says 'business' at once.

The supervisor, at least, should be on time, as an indication of her commitment. If delay is unavoidable, it is still important (especially in the early stages of supervision) not to neglect the opening procedures. It is not possible to lay down hard-and-fast rules about these, because they will depend on the personalities involved, on how well they know each other, whether they have been working together up to now on the same shift, and so on. The general principle, however, is to display interest in the staff member as a person, but to do so in such a way as to make possible a rapid move on to the supervision proper. Some people develop a stock phrase to do this – rather like the doctor's 'Now, what seems to be the trouble?' – but this depends on the situation.

The second level now comes into play: the *task level*. This is largely a matter of finding where the supervision is in relation to the contract, and is greatly aided if the recording system discussed later (p. 78) is adopted. Whether this approach is used or not, it helps to set the shape of the session if a few minutes are spent deciding which matters need attention today, and even how long ought to be spent on each of them. Although this sounds very formal and even impossible, the supervisor with some experience will soon find that she can make a fairly accurate prediction (at least 80 per cent of the time) about how long it will take to deal with specific items. Getting it wrong occasionally is no bad thing in any case; it shows that supervision is not simply a routinized activity.

## The middle

Most of this book is about the middle of the session, and so this will not receive much specific attention here. Considered from the point of view of the structure of the individual session, however, one major point does arise that is worthy of attention. This is the *controlled opening-up* of material, because it is in this area that many starting supervisors make mistakes, and, as always, it is a question of balance.

The middle of the session is where the items selected for discussion at the beginning are enlarged upon; this has to be done with an eye to the end of the session as well, to ensure that 'closure' can be obtained on the discussion (see below). Too little control, and the discussion becomes rambling and is likely to take in more and more material until it becomes unmanageable, and the session has to end with the feelings that nothing has been – or even can be – done about the situation. Too much control, and the staff member feels that he is not really being listened to, and will eventually clam up.

One way of representing the desired shape of the session is shown in *Figure 5*. Note that the 'exit' line from the session is

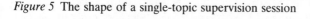

*Figure 5* The shape of a single-topic supervision session

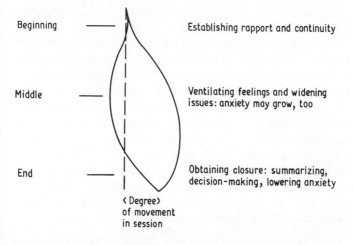

Beginning — Establishing rapport and continuity

Middle — Ventilating feelings and widening issues: anxiety may grow, too

End — Obtaining closure: summarizing, decision-making, lowering anxiety

‹ Degree›
of movement
in session

some way to the right of the 'entry' line – an indication of the progress made in that particular session. (For the sake of simplicity, the session is represented as if there were only one contract item under discussion.)

## The ending

The ending of the individual supervision session is of interest because of two factors, which affect each other closely: the issue of obtaining *closure*, and the phenomenon of the so-called *'doorknob syndrome'*.

'Closure' is a term used in several different senses in social work. In this case it refers to the need to close down the discussion after it has been opened up, to the extent that the material and feelings carried out of the session are manageable and will at the very least not adversely affect the work the staff member (or the supervisor) has to do after leaving the room. It is easy to get steamed up or confused or to experience a whole variety of other feelings in supervision, both good and bad. Working in group care is stressful enough and engenders enough feelings anyway, without adding to them unnecessarily; and supervision would hardly be contributing to the development of good practice within the establishment if staff members came out of it and took their feelings out on the clients. Seen in this light, it is desirable for staff to emerge in a fairly calm frame of mind.

On the other hand, feelings are very important, and it would be phoney to pretend that they could all be made to go away, and that people ought to leave in a state of bland serenity as if they had just completed an hour of meditation. More than that, feelings provide the energy behind change, and indeed behind the capacity to persist when things are getting tough; so it is vital that at the end of the session the staff member should leave with feelings at the right kind of level to motivate development. This certainly cannot be achieved by the supervisor glancing at her watch in the middle of a fascinating discussion and exclaiming, 'Good grief, is that the time? Sorry, that's all for today – see you next time!' Instead, about ten minutes or so need to be devoted at the end of the session to tying up the loose ends just as much as necessary, but no more.

In this ten minutes, either partner may attempt to summarize his or her understanding of what has gone on, checking it out with the other. Quick notes may be made for the supervision record, to be written up later; undertakings to do something specific before the next session (by either partner) can be clarified, and perhaps reminders may be passed on about forthcoming events between this session and the next one, thereby helping to make the transition between the world inside the supervision session and that outside. Therapy sessions in Transactional Analysis end with the ritual question to each member: 'Before we go, is there anything you want for your Child?' – although the jargon may not be appropriate, the sentiment certainly is. The supervisor may not ask such a question explicitly, but needs to be aware of the state of the staff member's feelings as he leaves, and to conclude on a note that, while not drawing the sting of any criticism that has to be voiced, encourages constructive feelings.

It is in this period, however, that one comes up against a phenomenon that can play havoc with schedules and ultimately with the contract and supervision as a whole. This is that psychologically, when the ending of a piece of interaction with another person is defined, people work back from it. The commonest expression of this is when, at the conclusion of some interview, a person stands with his hand on the door and says, 'Oh yes, there is just one other thing . . .' and this proves to be the most important item discussed in the entire interview. It is as if he could raise it only when he felt in control of the boundary of the interview – hand on door – and when he knew that there was not much time left to consider it in any detail. In slightly less obvious form, issues that come up under 'any other business' on committees may be more significant than the substantive items of the agenda.

Even when people protest that they really did not think of this topic until they were half-way through the door, it seems reasonable to suppose that there is a subconscious mechanism calculating that 'I can spend ten minutes discussing this, but I don't want it to go on for half an hour. So I will wait until there is ten minutes or less to go before I raise it.'

The supervisor is in a cleft stick. She may well not be able to dismiss the topic and make it wait until the next time; but if she accepts it, it will mean an over-hasty discussion of something that deserves better, and also a bypass of the contract. It is wise to make a note of the occurrence of the doorknob syndrome, and, if it happens too often, to point it out and thereafter refuse to be manipulated by it. Basically, it suggests that the supervision set-up, in particular the contract, is not an adequate container for some of the anxieties felt by the staff member. This cannot be dealt with by more structure or rules, but requires that the supervisor earn more trust. One way of doing this – assuming the supervisor *is* otherwise trustworthy – is to pay more attention to the scheduling of items within the session.

## THE CAREER OF SUPERVISION

So far in this chapter we have looked at the individual session. There is also a less obvious shape to the development of the supervision relationship in the form of supervision over a period of months and years. It is well to be aware of this, because otherwise a new supervisor can be disconcerted by the apparent deterioration in supervision at some stage; whole supervision programmes in establishments have foundered because of this.

Assuming that the introduction of supervision is welcomed by all concerned, the first few sessions are likely to be a *honeymoon*. The experience is novel, there is no shortage of things to talk about, neither partner has yet disappointed or let down the other. Sometimes this feeling lasts for only half a session, and if there has been a degree of suspicion about the introduction of the programme it may never be apparent at all. But if it does happen, the important thing is that neither partner – like honeymooning newly-weds – should be seduced by the feeling that it is going to last for ever, or indeed that it will be recaptured in its original form.

The honeymoon is followed by a period of *testing-out*, in most cases. The staff member begins to raise awkward issues that may test the patience, the confidentiality, and/or the skill of the supervisor. The supervisor probably does the same to the staff member, wondering how he will react if the pressure is put on a little more. Both partners are likely to leave sessions feeling stressed, and perhaps wondering whether it is all worthwhile. To anyone who works in group care, the pattern is familiar, since it duplicates closely the career of the new resident. Indeed, the sophisticated supervisor may even be able to make use of this parallel in supervision.

The next stage, however, is not as obvious in the residential setting as it is in supervision, where it can cause the whole programme to founder. This is the *doldrums*: a period, often about three months (roughly) after the beginning, when depression sets in because the supervision does not seem to be getting anywhere. It may not happen, but if it is going to happen it cannot be bypassed. It often coincides with the exhaustion of the first set of specific contract items, and is made worse if there has been a reluctance to move on from them. The novelty has worn off, the partners have got the measure of each other, and often there does not seem to be much left to talk about. There may well be grumblings in staff meetings about supervision being a waste of time, appointments will tend to be missed, and the whole programme may sink lower and lower in the level of priorities of the establishment. The supervisor may be tempted to let the sessions become more and more managerial in nature, and to back off from engaging with the staff member as a person in role.

There is no cure, as such. Given time, and committed professional persistence, the doldrums will pass; but there is not much point in trying to jazz supervision up with more exercises, or by varying its format, to make the blues go away. Occasionally I have worked with establishments that have decided to adopt supervision on a six-month trial basis; and it has never survived to six months. Either an initial decision has to be made that the programme will be permanent, or, if an experimental period *must* be chosen, it has to be shorter than about three months.

Once the doldrums have been navigated, supervision settles down into a pattern of *taken-for-granted naturalness*, in which it is just part of 'the way we do things here', and as such is accepted by new members of the community and old-stagers alike. There is a danger in this. It can become similar to the kind of institutionalization that besets the long-term resident, so that the programme which emerges into this fourth stage bears little relation to what was embarked upon with such enthusiasm not so long before. Periodic review, and the professional discipline of the supervisor, should be able to overcome this.

On the whole, it seems that all the people being supervised will go through the above stages, roughly together if they started at the same time. But even in the fourth stage, there will be ups and downs – and a repetitious cycle of testing and doldrums – although these may happen at different times for different people. In part they stem from learning plateaux (see p. 149), and in part from external factors in and outside the establishment.

The evidence for these stages comes not from scientific surveys, but from 'clinical' – or, if you like, anecdotal – experience. I include these observations in order that supervisors, and their supervisees, should not be thrown by encountering changes that are not really understood. There is however a danger that by describing such changes I may be setting up a self-fulfilling prophecy, and so the reader is urged to test the value of the observations rigorously against her own experience.

# 7 Recording and Monitoring

The first question is, Why record supervision? After all, supervision itself is time-consuming, and all concerned are busy people, so there needs to be a good reason for taking additional time to record it.

Recording in itself is useful for two reasons:

(1) The act of making notes on an activity is an aid to reflection on it.
(2) It helps to ensure continuity between sessions.

More than that, however, a recording scheme that is well thought out enables you to

(3) monitor and evaluate the effectiveness of supervision as practised.

## EVALUATING THE EFFECTIVENESS OF SUPERVISION

This third objective leads to a different focus. What is required is not so much an account of what goes on inside the supervision session, but a means of evaluating its impact *outside* the session in the real world of practice.

Many people are a little uncomfortable with the idea of evaluation. They are familiar with the problem that methods of social work evaluation have tended to be so crude, and to ignore so many significant variables, that their results have distorted practice. Either the research misrepresents the practice, focusing on some features to the exclusion of others – usually choosing concrete, measurable items at the cost of more important but vaguer aspects like the quality of relationships – or other people are wont to draw unwarranted conclusions from the research, and to devalue parts of the job that practitioners think important. The challenge, therefore, is to devise ways to assess the effectiveness of supervision, both in general and in particular terms, that are fair, do justice to the complexity of the task, and are also worth the effort.

**Evaluating the programme in general**

There is no 'objective' way to assess the effectiveness of supervision in general, because it is not possible to hold constant all the other variables likely to affect outcomes. Such evaluation is more certain to be achieved by more subjective methods, such as by asking for opinions on its effectiveness at staff meetings at regular but not too frequent intervals. This does not have to be haphazard. It is possible to devise questionnaires – perhaps including rating scales – that can be used to get feedback in a systematic form, which can then be used to modify the supervision programme.

*Figure 6* is a specimen evaluation questionnaire of this kind. The 'trick' in the design of such material is to meet the needs of both the people filling it in and the people who will use the information it yields. The superiority of a questionnaire over simply opening up a topic for discussion in a staff meeting lies in the fact that everybody is likely to fill in the questionnaire (particularly if it is both simple and anonymous), whereas not everyone is equally likely to express their views in a discussion. Also, writing their views down concisely helps people to focus their attention on the subject. Filling in the questionnaire first and then having a general discussion gives the best of both worlds; and while unpopular opinions may be 'censored' by group pressure within the staff meeting, once they are written down they have the same weight as everyone else's.

The questionnaire provides a device to enable people to say simply and clearly what they want to say. Many official and commercial forms are designed purely for the benefit of those who commission them – to assess your eligibility for credit, for example. In this case, however, the respondents' needs also

*Figure 6* Specimen evaluation questionnaire

| | | | | |
|---|---|---|---|---|
| (1) Generally speaking, how useful have you found supervision? | *Not at all useful* | *Quite useful* | *Very useful* | |
| (2) How much difference has having supervision made to your own practice, if any? | *None at all* | *A little* | *Quite a lot* | *A great deal* |
| (3) Do you think the present frequency of supervision is: | *not often enough?* | *about right?* | *too often?* | |
| (4) Do you think the supervision sessions are: | *too long?* | *about right?* | *not long enough?* | |

(5) How useful have you found the following aspects of supervision?

| *Discussion of*: | *Very useful* | *Quite useful* | *Not at all useful* | *Has not happened* |
|---|---|---|---|---|
| Individual clients' needs | | | | |
| Approaches to care for clients | | | | |
| Procedures of the establishment | | | | |
| Specific incidents | | | | |
| Personal feelings about the job | | | | |
| Personal feelings about clients | | | | |
| Working as part of a team etc. | | | | |

(6) Have you any suggestions about how supervision might be developed further?

(7) Any other comments

have to be considered. So questions go in either if you can think of a good reason for making use of the answers, or in order to enable staff to give a full view of supervision from their experience. The name of the individual staff member may well be irrelevant, and there is no need to ask for it. If he wants to identify himself as an individual, he can write it in.

Probably the simplest practical form of such an evaluation questionnaire is one that asks for an item of 'good news' about supervision and one of 'bad news'. The slight additional focus provided by such questions gets beyond the mere 'What do you think about supervision?' – which is so vague as to leave staff with little idea of the kind of response required, and may also give the impression that no one really knows what questions to ask. However, you may wish to be more specific, and you can choose any level of generality, down to asking about outcomes for individuals in specific areas. See *Figure 7*.

If the questionnaire is very specific, recognize that individual contracts may not have allowed for some areas to be covered, and make sure that there are more general questions that enable staff to say what *they* want to say as well.

There is no point in undertaking such evaluation too soon. Supervision has its own career (see Chapter 6, 'The Supervision Session'), and surveying it in the doldrums will mainly reflect that stage, rather than a fair account of the whole programme. So leave it for at least six months before attempting any formal evaluation, and perhaps longer if supervision is offered only, say, one a month.

### Using the information

Having received the information, supplemented with verbal comments, collate it and get the general picture. Resolve to respond to the critical points that emerge. They are *not* votes of no confidence in the supervisor (usually); they are statements about the 'fit', or lack of it, between what is on offer and what the staff can make use of. As such, they need to be taken seriously as pointers to further action, even when they contradict the advice in this guide.

*Figure 7* Part of detailed monitoring questionnaire, to check material covered in supervision, and to set requirements for contract revision (relates to a home for mentally handicapped children)

This questionnaire is intended to help us summarize where you are in relation to some of the things that you may have been discussing in supervision. Please tick in the appropriate column, and make any further comments you like.

|  | *Not discussed* | *Needs more discussion* | *Fully understood* | *Comments* |
|---|---|---|---|---|
| Understanding how each child's capabilities are assessed | | | | |
| Understanding treatment/training programmes for each child | | | | |
| Understanding our philosophy on:<br>– discipline<br>– mealtimes<br>– hygiene<br>– visitors<br>– sex education<br>– parental involvement | | | | |
| Being able to carry out key-worker responsibilities in respect of:<br>– liaison with other professionals<br>– liaison with parents<br>– making progress reports<br>– monitoring care programme<br>– aids, special procedures, etc. | | | | |

However, it is only half the story to find out that staff enjoy supervision, or that they think it is a waste of time. The questions should include some that will help to differentiate between the task-related and the person-related elements of the supervision process. It is possible that staff hate supervision but none the less find it useful, and that its task-effectiveness comes first – although, if supervision is to provide support as well, some sense of enjoyment or satisfaction is a fairly close second. The other half of the story comes from evidence of the pay-offs for the investment of time.

Throughout this book I have held out the carrot that supervision promises more time back than is put into it. Is this true? Can the Head of Home identify specific areas of delegation that have become possible over the last six months? If they can be identified, have they in fact been delegated? If not, why not? In short, has it become easier to find the time to practise supervision, and has your job become easier as a result? If it has not, and there are no other major factors, then you need to think seriously about whether supervision is effective. Don't just think about it by yourself; talk to your own supervisor about it.

## MONITORING INDIVIDUAL SUPERVISION

The other area of evaluation is the matter of the progress made by each individual staff member through the supervision offered, and this cannot be assessed primarily through the experience of the sessions themselves. Although it is an almost necessary by-product that supervision becomes more comfortable, open, and indeed interesting as time goes by, its impact on practice is much more important. This aspect needs to become the focus of the monitoring activity.

There may well be resistance to such evaluation of practice, and there are two major reasons for it. The first is that it smacks too much of putting staff through hoops; and the second that it constitutes a sort of unofficial appraisal, which may have implications for promotion and career development, even though supervision is supposed to be confidential. The proposal to evaluate in this way therefore requires sensitive handling and may be expected once more to raise issues of trust between staff member and supervisor.

### The supervisee as monitor

In the light of all this, coupled with the time-consuming nature of separate evaluation procedures, it makes sense to adopt an approach to evaluation that is natural rather than imposed. Such an approach is likely to be experienced as more comfortable for both supervisor and staff member, and hence is more likely to stand the test of time. Fortunately, the existence of the supervision contract provides an ideal basis for such evaluation, and moreover enables most of it to be carried out by the staff member rather than by the supervisor. If the system is set up properly, there is a great deal of benefit to be derived from this option.

In the first place, it shares the load more sensibly. The supervisor may be working with half a dozen members of staff, and would therefore have six reports to write if she were to do it herself. Each staff member, on the other hand, has only one to do.

Second, it helps the staff member to keep the supervision work in mind, in the period between sessions, if he has to pay attention to a monitoring programme.

Third, the fact that the staff member rather than the supervisor is keeping the record allows the system adopted to pay more attention to what is most important about the monitoring programme: what happens between the sessions. Unless the supervisor and staff member actually work together a great deal of the time, some of the staff member's activity will be invisible to the supervisor, and so she would have to rely on his own reporting anyway. So why not make use of it more effectively?

Fourth, in the not uncommon event that the staff member needs to gain some experience in recording and reporting, this exercise is a useful source of practice.

Fifth, the fact that the staff member is in control minimizes the kind of suspicion mentioned earlier.

Against the method, however, is the usually unspoken question of the extent to which one can trust the staff member to represent accurately what happened both within and between sessions. If there are doubts on this score, the supervisor can always keep skeletal notes for a few weeks as a check, until reassured.

### Designing a monitoring system

The format has to be as simple as possible to operate (the simpler it is, the more likely it will get used), but also able to do justice to the complexity of the material handled. There are many ways of satisfying these criteria; one of them is to follow the format below – which works best with a separate sheet of paper for each contract item, or a separate column for each item on the same sheet.

(1) Contract item.
(2) Work on that item planned at last session.
(3) Steps towards (2) achieved.
(4) Obstacles to the completion of (2).
(5) Matters arising for discussion at next session.

Note that items (1) and (2) are the only parts that refer directly to the supervision session itself, although part (5) helps to set the agenda for the next one. Sections (3) and (4) are concerned with what is done (or not done) in practice, and the ground covered by those sections should always equal or exceed section (2).

The procedure for the use of such a format is as follows.

(1) During the supervision session, notes are made on (1) and (2), as part of the summary in the final few minutes. (1) will not require much attention, since it will already have been defined as part of the contract, unless it is a new item.
(2) Note, however, that the work identified in (2) needs to be

specific enough to be reported on in the terms of (3) and (4), and also to be practicable in the period between the sessions.

(3) A day or two before the next session, the supervisee writes up (3) and (4) – and probably (5) – and passes the report back to the supervisor. The latter reads it so that she can prepare herself for the session, and makes any necessary notes, possibly adding to (5).

(4) At the subsequent session, review of (3) and (4) and then more examination of (5) form the agenda for the work on that contract item for the session.

It may seem that section (4) is not strictly necessary; after all, the difference between (2) (what ought to be achieved) and (3) (what was achieved) must equal (4) (what was not achieved). However, identifying and filling in (4) before the supervision session is a useful exercise. It may suggest ways in which that material could in fact be dealt with, or more likely it will show that something is wrong with the formulation of (2) or even of the contract item in the first place. Section (5) is, as it were, a feedback loop, facilitating corrections in earlier stages of the planning process. (See the planning diagram in the Introduction, *Figure 1*.)

Such a pattern fits well enough for 'cold shower' supervision, and also suits therapeutic programmes for individual residents – but does it work for 'warm bath', supportive supervision? After all, if the contract provides for the staff member to get things off his chest, or even to talk about external pressures that are making his work difficult, are there likely to be specific pieces of work planned as a result of such discussions? If there are, it will not necessarily be the staff member who has to do them. The supervisor too has responsibility for working between sessions, and there is no reason why her commitment should not be recorded and monitored just as much as the staff member's. Even if there is little identifiable 'work' to be done in section (2) (you may decide that all you can do is wait for something to happen), it can still be noted, and the outcomes included in (3) or (4) as appropriate.

**Who keeps the reports?**

The remaining question is, Who keeps the reports? Here again, the answer is straightforward: the staff member. It is his supervision, after all. If there is a confidentiality component in the supervision contract, he will feel more secure if he is the person who holds the records, and he can take them home or do what he wants with them, as long as he keeps them. If the supervisor is left with the records on a number of staff, she has the problem of what to do with them; does she keep them in the filing cabinet where they may be available to a number of people, or in the safe, or where?

This also removes one of the pressures to which supervisors sometimes find themselves subject, and that some staff fear: to make use of supervision material in periodical appraisals of staff. If it is expected that this will be the case, then it needs to be provided for in the initial contract, and there are arguments on both sides. On the whole, I believe that it is preferable to keep supervision and appraisal separate. Ideally, they should not be practised by the same person, because the appraisal 'reaches back' into the supervision session and keeps the staff member on the defensive. On the other hand, those concerned with evaluating staff performance are entitled to claim that if the information from ongoing supervision is available it is silly not to include such a valuable source in the appraisal process itself. This is a difficult point to answer, except to say that appraisal is designed to be an assessment of performance that is as objective as possible. What the staff member does is the important thing – not why he does it, or how he arrives at it. If the staff member holds the supervision record, then he is entitled to furnish what material he wishes for appraisal purposes, since some of it will be relevant and some not. If he does not wish to show it to anyone, then that is his right.

It is interesting to note the contrast between this way of thinking about files and records and who has 'natural' access to them, and that normally applied to residents. The latter may not even know that their version of 'appraisal' – the case conference or statutory review – is taking place.

Despite all the above, many supervisors will want to keep their own notes on supervision. If so, then they should be open to the staff member. The big problem with theoretically 'open' files is that they spawn another set of closed files behind them, which are entirely unofficial, unaccountable, and even gossipy. Such notes have no place in supervision (or anywhere else), and should not be set up.

ADDITIONAL METHODS

There are occasions when it may be desirable to supplement routine written recording with other techniques, for particular purposes.

The simplest additional resource is the use of graphics, in the form of large sheets of paper, written or drawn on with felt-tip markers, which can be pinned up session by session. They may record the development of a discussion, using, for example, Buzan's technique (Buzan 1974). They may have lists on them, to be added to session by session. They may be diagrams, or keywords. However they are used, their reappearance in each session emphasizes the continuity of supervision, and they provide an additional channel of communication between supervisor and staff member.

The most obvious use of audio or video recording is for training purposes. They are methods that allow you to stand back and get some idea of your own performance from the outside. You soon forget about the presence of microphone or camera; initial self-consciousness gives way to absorption in the task of supervision. Reviewing the result can be both fascinating and disconcerting; and both supervisor and staff member can learn a great deal about how they present themselves. The method does have the great disadvantage of requiring 'real-time' playback; i.e. it takes as long to view the session as it took to have it in the first place. However, there is no need to watch (or listen to) all of it. There is often more benefit to be derived from reviewing five minutes or less, and subjecting it to a fairly detailed analysis, than from re-running the whole thing and not having sufficient time to discuss it afterwards. The onus, however, is on whoever wants to use such a method to prove that it is necessary – partly because of the extent to which it can be a distraction, and partly because the formulation of such a case demands that its use be thought through properly, and therefore that more effective use is made of the exercise when it does occur.

An article by Peter Hawkins in *Community Care* also points out how recordings can be used by supervisors to map out how much of their time they are putting into which areas of supervision, and whether anything is being left out (Hawkins 1982). Since telling what is not happening is often more difficult than telling what is, the occasional use of such techniques has much to recommend it.

One final point about recording technique. Anything badly recorded is tiring and distracting to listen to or watch. So record only if it can be done well. Don't rely on built-in microphones on cameras or in tape-recorders. Don't put microphones on those little table stands, where they may get jogged and banged and may pick up all kinds of extraneous noise. Get hold of a proper stand, or use tie-clip microphones. If you can record in stereo, so much the better; particularly in a room where the acoustics are 'boomy', the slightly different stereo images will cancel out some of the boom and give a clearer image, even when played back in mono.

When the material is finished with, rub it out.

# Part Two

# 8 Topics of Supervision

After setting up supervision and drawing up the contract, it would seem that the remainder is plain sailing. We know what to talk about, so now we simply go ahead and talk about it. That is so, but this chapter is designed to draw attention to the fact that there are different ways of talking about people and occurrences in group-care settings, and that some of these ways are more helpful than others. What is special about supervision, after all, is talking about people and things – which are already talked about elsewhere – only in the kind of way that contributes to the development of good practice. Even then there is no particular virtue in taking time out for an hour a week to talk 'professionally', whilst continuing to act non-professionally for the rest of the time. This special kind of talking is intended to have some impact at least in the wider world of the establishment. Sometimes it may even have an impact in the lives of clients after or outside care. So mumbling the pieties of whatever passes for the social work ideology of the day is not enough; supervision has to take account of the way staff presently think, feel, and act, and of the impact of that for good or ill as well.

## INCIDENTS

One of the characteristics of residential and day-care work is that life consists of a series of incidents that call for rapid intervention and solution. Two handicapped adults start arguing about whose record goes on the stereo next; staff have to sort it out. An elderly resident has a stroke and has to go to hospital. A young lad comes in stumbling all over the place and bumping into things, and a giggling child behind says he's been sniffing glue. An old lady complains that someone has been nicking her knickers. From the serious to the trivial, from questions of suspicion and strong feelings to simple administrative responses, the staff on duty have to *do* something, and do it quickly. This leads to a kind of rough justice in residential establishments, in which getting the matter sorted out is more important than the fine distinctions of guilt and innocence; and also to a distinct attitude of mind amongst socialized residential workers about 'what *ought* to be done'. (Technically, this 'rough justice' is a shame-culture; for further discussion see Atherton 1983.) Often staff do not seem to be very comfortable with examining what *is* actually going on in a particular situation, but more with what needs to be done to put it right again.

There is nothing wrong with this approach in itself; indeed, it is essential to effective performance and the running of an establishment. But it has its faults as well as its virtues, and sometimes it needs to be counterbalanced, particularly when this *pre*scriptive approach (as distinct from the *de*scriptive approach found amongst fieldworkers – equally essential, but equally limited) becomes a matter of 'recipes'. A recipe is a way of working that comes down to 'Whenever so and so happens, I always'. Sometimes the recipe is spelt out – usually when old hands are initiating young staff. More often it is detected first by the outsider, who may say that a staff member seems to act *as if* a certain stimulus was always to be followed by a certain response. And some recipes are enshrined in the procedures of the establishment, such as fire drill.

Recipes have their uses (particularly in fire drill and other emergency procedures); but they suffer from treating every occurrence of a certain kind, such as every inter-resident argument, as if it were like every other occurrence of the same kind. This leads to the insensitive handling of situations and to injustice and resentment, even when the recipe seems to be sanctioned by the rules of the establishment. If only the staff member would look beyond the situation that immediately confronts him, he could arrive at a more sophisticated response, because he would see that each situation is different even when it *looks* exactly like some of the others. This often seems to be a counsel of perfection, because we know that staff work under pressure, and cannot spend hours working out the background to a trivial incident involving two clients when there are ten others who need attention at the same time. But it is possible to help staff to be more flexible in their responses if they are given the tools to think with, and supervision is the ideal setting in which to do it.

One effective supervision tool is to milk the incident for all that it is worth in supervision:

– What happened?
– Of that account of what happened, what is indisputable fact and what is interpretation? (Interpretation is essential).
– What does that interpretation say about your way of looking at incidents?
– What preceded what happened?
– What caused it? (Not always the same thing.)
– What were the ripples afterwards? What were the effects on the residents not directly involved?
– How was it handled?
– In what other ways could it have been handled, and what might have been their outcomes?
– What were the hidden messages in the way it was handled?
– Did those messages help or hinder the work you are trying to do with the clients involved? With the bystanders?
– Is it likely to recur? Is it a variation on a theme elsewhere in the establishment?
– What does it say about the life of the group; about the structure of the establishment; about the personalities and problems of individual residents and staff?

(The above is not a check-list of questions to ask, but an indication of the kind of enquiry one can make into the simplest incident, good or bad.)

In short, the emphasis is on the *de*scription of the incident rather than the *pre*scription of response, in order to uncover some of its complexities. No one can analyse a situation in that way while it is happening or in the immediate aftermath; but repeated practice leads to a more open way of thinking and the consideration of more options for action – even if staff end up doing the same old thing in the end (which is not always wrong).

## Alternative accounts

A useful exercise for supervision as well as training events is the generation of alternative accounts of what may be going on in a simple situation. The more stuck in a rut the staff member is, the more difficult he will find it to produce different explanations of the situation.

The exercise works like this:

(1) Describe the bare bones of an incident to the staff member. Keep the incident as simple as possible. Provide the necessary information but no more. At first, it is better to pick an incident in which the people are not known to the staff members; this helps to avoid labelling and taken-for-granted ideas. If the technique does not appear to work, this is almost invariably because the supervisor makes the situation too complicated. The simplest is the best; e.g. 'Tracey complained to you of having a tummy-ache this morning'.

(2) Get the staff member to produce as many interpretations as possible of what the incident might mean. Do not criticize or rule any of them out of court; list them all on a large sheet of paper that you can both see.

(3) When the staff member can produce no more accounts, go through those listed, looking at the kind of intervention or response that might be demanded by each of them. Make a separate list of these.

(4) Examine what might be the consequences of each of the possible kinds of intervention identified. Be sure to cover all of them.

(5) Resist the temptation or the request to give the 'right' answer at the end. You may want to say what actually happened, but make it clear that there is no guarantee that the response employed was the best one.

Several variations are possible on the theme:

(1)  You may wish to pay attention to how many accounts the staff member can produce; the more in a rut she is, the fewer she will manage. Encourage her to produce more each time you try it.

(2)  Look at the accounts generated; what do they say about the staff member? Do they focus on any themes that have been 'read into' the situation? Are there any obvious ones conspicuous by their absence? Supply these, and find out why they did not occur to her, or were not voiced.

(3)  In the shift from description to action, value-judgements are inevitable. Work with the staff member on the assumptions she is making in suggesting courses of action, and what they say about her values.

In routine supervision the approach can be applied to incidents already mentioned by the staff member. It is best not to be too critical of the final outcomes, but simply to point out that there *are* alternative accounts, and that short-term 'success' in 'dealing with' the situation is not the only goal.

**Behind the interpretation**

It is often in the discussion of incidents rather than of individual residents that the biases, labels, and prejudices (for good or ill) of the staff begin to emerge. Look out for what the staff member says about herself as she describes the incident. Is there an exclusive focus on 'problems'? Incidents can be good as well as bad, fun as well as crises. Are interpretations of behaviour one-sided, black or white, or do they indicate favouritism? Is the staff member able to make the working distinction between 'normal' incapacity or naughtiness – to be expected in any person at that age, stage, or social situation – on the one hand, and distinctive problematic incapacity on the other? In child care, all children are naughty and nasty and cruel at some time or other; any child removed from home may be expected to be upset and angry about it, to say the least. It is only the frame of reference of social work that tends to see normal naughtiness as evidence of a deep-seated underlying pathology (see Tutt 1974). The problem comes when the normal and the pathological coexist; how do you sort them out?

Such discussion not only helps to counter recipes and stereotyped thinking, but it also has another effect, particularly of value to the tired and flattened staff member; it helps to increase the sense of *wonder*. After one session with a small group working on these lines, a member commented that it was like beginning to see things in colour rather than black and white. To think that all this was going on in what looked like such a simple situation! So much description of what happens in our work setting is clogged with standardized reactions; we say that a child is 'cheeky' or even 'insolent', but vast assumptions about the social structure and the nature of authority are contained in those judgements. We comment that a mentally handicapped resident told a lie, but never wonder at the complexities of understanding relationships and adjusting to them, which are contained in this everyday interaction. Like everyone who works in a situation that is sometimes unpleasant, we become inured to things that would shock, scare, or otherwise upset a lay person. Having battened down the hatches on our vulnerability and hence sensitivity, we do not realize that occasionally it is safe to open them a little – or that, if we do open them, the world outside is not only frightening or nauseating, but also fascinating and moving. It is possible to sustain both a professional distance (and even the painfully acquired cynicism and distrust that are often needed in social work) together with sensitivity and openness.

INDIVIDUAL CLIENTS

Supervision, unlike case conferences and statutory reviews, can concentrate more informally on the day-to-day life and experience of the clients 'in the round', without having to restrict itself to problem areas. I am against inexhaustible discussion to the extent that the client disappears in a welter of complexes, quotients, inadequacies, and labels. The effect of such discussion is to lose sight of his individuality and uniqueness, and this is the opposite of the approach that supervision tries to cultivate. Although there are occasions when you have to help a staff member to regain some degree of professional distance from a person about whom they cannot be at all objective, the main trust of supervisory discussions of individual clients is in the opposite direction. With the support of supervision, a staff member should be able to tolerate seeing each client as a real person, distinguishable from the crowd, and worthy of a bit of unfairness. Since the client 'out there' is in fact real enough, the focus of attention is the image of the client existing inside the staff member's head. You might ask:

- What does the world look like to this person?
- How does he see being in this place?
- What role does the cast you (the staff member) in?
- How does he relate to that role?
- What does he feel he can and cannot do?
- What does he feel safest with?
- What does 'safety' mean to him?
- What is he most threatened by?
- What does 'threat' mean to him?
- What appears trivial to you and me, but matters to him?
- What are his fantasies and hopes?
- What are his memories like?
- What are his tastes?
- What are his talents?
- How does he affect those who get close to him?

Again, these questions are not a check-list, but just suggestions of what you might ask to make a client more live. It is important to avoid jargon, and to express things in language that the client might understand, even if he would not use it. The reason for this is to permit checking of ideas (very subtly, or course), and to avoid the construction of vast theoretical edifices bearing no relation to the way the client experiences the world. Jargon is a reflection of 'black-box' thinking; it is a vocabulary created for a specific purpose within a specific occupational group, and it obscures what lies outside the concerns of that group as much as it illuminates what lies inside. This kind of supervision exercise is concerned with doing justice to as much as possible of the whole person, not just the client-in-relation-to-Social-Services-and-this-establishment.

Some staff baulk at this kind of exercise. Some maintain that speculation is dangerous and may do a disservice to the client if it is wrong. Some say that it is impossible to know how anyone else thinks anyway, and therefore futile to try. Some regard it as unscientific. Some admit that if they thought about what some of the clients had been through in their upbringing – or what it might feel like to know that the only people who appear to care for you do so at least in part because they are paid to – then they would be unable to do their jobs. But to deny yourself the freedom to wonder about the inner world of the residents is to take the first step to regarding them as if they did not *have* an inner world of feelings. What might be the feeling that drives a girl to abscond, with nowhere to go and no one to go to, and in spite of the knowledge that absconding solves nothing but makes things worse? Her reasoning may appear meaningless, but it must be good enough for her, or she would not act on it. What might that reasoning be? Or what is it that makes Mrs Jones so resistant to stimulation, and yet so ready to grumble about having nothing to do all day? Is it only her anger that keeps her alive?

If the staff can grapple with these issues in supervision, there is a chance that they may be interested enough to listen to people in such a way that those people will tell them the parts of the answer that they do know for themselves.

THE EFFECTS OF CLIENTS ON EACH OTHER

We never see clients purely as individuals. Part of their personhood comes from their interaction with others, and the often-heard 'In a group he's a menace, but just get him on his own, and he's fine' points to the variability, not only of behaviour, but of attitudes and values within different social situations. But that statement suggests that the person in question is somehow more 'real' on his own, and is 'corrupted' by the group. This is phoney. We have to live with people all the time, and how we behave when we are with them is just as worthy of judgement as is our behaviour when we are on our own (see Douglas 1983).

Within the group, norms reinforce certain kinds of behaviour and lead to the extinction of others. More important, people learn to see themselves as they are mirrored by the perceptions of other members of the group. They internalize all that, and it becomes part of themselves. But how much freedom does the group give to a newcomer to find a congenial role, to 'be herself'? To what extent does she have to take up the only vacant slot? Can she, does she, change her group?

- What are the norms of the group(s) of clients?
- To what extent do they understand those norms?
- How are they enforced?
- What kind of leadership is there in these groups?
- What other roles are there besides that of leader?
- What roles does this group need to have filled in order to continue to exist?
- How does it exert pressure on its members?
- What other sub-groups are there amongst the residents?
- How stable are they?
- Who is in which group at the moment?
- What do they represent of the life of the whole?
- Are they constructive or destructive, in your view?
- What part does the staff play in creating these sub-groups (deliberately or accidentally)?

It is rather like training a naturalist to see the interaction and the interdependence amongst the denizens of a small clearing in the forest; in other words, we are trying to get at the ecology of the residents' world. This ecology always exists, even in the apparently stagnant pool of a lounge full of old people sitting round the walls.

What follows from the above is an appreciation that it is not possible to intervene in the situation of one person without affecting all the others in some way or other, usually in a way that we do not understand and cannot predict. If a group of boys has been troublesome for some time and I choose to 'make an example' of one or two of them, is that likely to bring the rest back into line because of the fear of what might happen to them? Or is it likely to increase the overall level of resentment of the staff among the group as a whole? Are the punished troublemakers ostracized from the group because they have got into trouble, or do they become leaders with the status of rebels? Alternatively, does 'making an example' have no effect whatsoever? I'm against making an example of anyone, but all of these consequences, and more, are possible alternatives and they are difficult to determine.

The consequences of an action may be related as much to the member of staff involved as to the particular intervention – a fact that we recognize intuitively when we say, '*You* tell them. They'll take it from you.' What staff *represent* to the residents often speaks louder than what they *do*; and it is hard for even an experienced member of staff to accept that there is absolutely no way she is going to get through to Jenny, no matter how hard she tries. It may have nothing at all to do with personality, or skill, or intentions; it may be that no one who is white (or who has a posh accent, or once said she did not like a certain pop group, or supports the wrong football team) has any chance.

The ideology of child care tries to treat children as individuals with individual problems (Bramham 1980) and therefore comes to see their own groups as inimical to the 'treatment' process. Some establishments go to great lengths to make sure that groups created and defined by the staff are the only ones that thrive within the establishment. Children's own chosen groupings are regarded as dangerous. Others ignore children's groupings and see them as irrelevant. With other client groups, there is a tendency to believe that somehow the group processes do not happen as they do in the world at large, perhaps because dependence on staff is so overwhelming as to swamp other processes *when staff are present.* But try to change the culture of a hostel for mentally handicapped adults, or of an old people's home, and the power of the resistance shows the power of the group.

Whatever the perspective and policy of the establishment, an understanding of the group process is central. Supervision is an appropriate forum to get some distance from it and to develop skills in observing and interpreting it.

However, it is important not to get carried away, as sometimes both staff member and supervisor are, by an appealing hypothesis. Every idea must be subject to testing; a useful hypothesis will either reveal some idea of the evidence that will strengthen or disprove it, or have some predictive value, so that you can test out whether the expected outcome occurs or not. Except under conditions of crisis, when decisions may be forced however incomplete the evidence, it is wise to treat all such ideas formulated in supervision as strictly provisional, and not to act on them until you have some moral certainty of their accuracy and usefulness.


ROUTINES

The structure of routine tasks in a home is a matter for managerial policy, and as such is not most effectively dealt with in supervision (except in the case of new staff members, who need not only to know how things are done, but also to understand the reasons). But there is an institutional aspect to the supervision process, and in social work there is no clear-cut distinction between 'management' and 'professional' practice. After all, the basis of residential social work is the management of the living environment of other people.

Routines are far from a purely technical matter. Their management raises questions of values, and in this respect they become material for supervision. When carried through with conviction, a particular way of handling a routine event such as bedtime or bathtime can communicate a great deal to a resident, for better or for worse. In supervision, staff may well want to query and explore the way certain things are done.

With a good account of the reasons and the philosophy, staff are more likely to be able to internalize them, and thus make the most of the opportunities that the routines offer. Not only does this help the clients, but it also enables staff to add an extra dimension to their work, and thus to avoid being bored stiff (and if staff are bored, this gives a terrible message to the residents).

The problem is that routine aspects of the work tend to be neglected and regarded as sub-professional. Even much of the recent writing on residential work carries this implication. (See, for example, CCETSW 1973; Jones 1978; in the latter the 'residential community' does not appear to be valued in its own right, but as a 'setting' for another kind of activity called 'social work'.) If this is felt to be the case, then a large proportion of the work done by residential staff is written off as of no great importance, except in so far as it is necessary to enable more exciting and glamorous things to be done. This betrays a set of assumptions about clients' needs that is unwarranted, particularly the idea that more is communicated by words than by actions.

In its unsophisticated form, this model suggests that bathing, for example, is important only for hygienic and functional reasons. In a more sophisticated form, it concedes that bathtime may present an opportunity for a client to talk to a member of staff in private and whilst sharing a common activity. Neither view takes any account of the problems of organizing bathing so as to minimize its institutional connotations, nor of the shock of having regular baths to many clients who come into care, nor of the opportunities for conveying something important to a client offered by consistent and sensitive attention to intimate personal needs. Do clients have a choice as to whether they have a bath or not, or its frequency? Does the procedure go on all day – as often happens in old people's homes – or, with younger residents, start immediately after tea, so that a succession of people emerge from the bathroom in dressing-gowns to sit around for the rest of the evening? Or is it a mad rush just before bedtime, so that there can be no privacy and no time for a meditative soak? And how are such issues decided by the management of the home? Very often it is administrative convenience that determines the procedure, because the possible value-judgements involved either go unrecognized or prove too difficult to resolve. (For immensely detailed discussion of the rationale of routines, see Bettelheim 1950.)

There are also those routines that become rituals, so that their predictability becomes a source of security in a chaotic world. (Security is something to rebel against as well as something to wallow in.)

- Why do we do things the way we do?
- What messages to the clients are implicit in our procedures?
- What effects do they have on individual clients?
- On groups within the home?
- What routine procedures do you, as a staff member, tend to fudge?
- Why? What are the effects of such short cuts?
- What routines have to be handled extra sensitively because of their significance to residents?
- What does sensitive handling look like?
- Does it differ from resident to resident?
- Are there any necessary procedures that diminish the dignity of the individual?
- How might they be improved?

One difficulty of this area of supervision is that routines are often the heritage of history, and sometimes even Heads of Home do not really know why they are handled as they are. Some procedure was instituted in response to special circumstances in the past, and its residue persists to this day, often unchallenged. As time goes by, such routines acquire symbolic significance, and become part of the identity of the establishment; to challenge them therefore hits at relatively deep feelings, which people are not always able to articulate to themselves. So they take refuge in all kinds of improbable explanations, which really come down to the fact that they just cannot conceive of doing things differently. The supervisor needs to examine himself on this front before he takes on this aspect of supervision, or else he will end up mystifying both himself and other staff when it comes up.

## Handling the routines

Whatever the framework of routine organization, the actual administration can vary considerably between staff members. That bath-and-bed procedure which starts immediately after tea can be handled sensitively or insensitively, its opportunities exploited or ignored. An approach to mealtimes designed to give value to the social and communal significance of eating together can still be ruined by crude handling. This stems sometimes from a basic ignorance of the rationale and sometimes from a wider kind of ignorance, which takes no account of the duty of the staff to help clients to learn and function at as high a level as possible:

> 'I just thought that it was so inefficient and messy, what with them passing the serving dishes from one to another across the table. They always knock over a glass of water or spill the gravy or custard, you know. And then the tablecloths have to be washed again, if you have them, that is. So we have been using the formica-topped tables without a cloth on them, and Cook plates the meat and I do the veg. for them. . . . They still get what they ask for.'

The above statement sounds like the basis for a whole series of supervision sessions on its own. The fact that the food gets served efficiently may be missing almost the whole point; the method was devised to encourage sharing and to develop co-operation between clients on the same table. Built into the method was the costing that a few spills and spoiled tablecloths matter less than the opportunity to learn. (However, the method the staff member describes is also consciously used in other settings for other, equally sophisticated reasons.) Here we are beginning to move into the area that is of central importance for the development of staff practice: the *fit* between what the staff member is and feels able to do, on the one hand, and what is required of him as part of the residential community, on the other. In relation to routines, the question is, Can this staff member carry through the procedure as we do it here, faithful not only to the letter but also to the spirit, and knowing why he is doing if this way? If not, why not? And what can be done about it?

## STAFF ROLES

This is the second area of fit between staff member and establishment, in this case to do with an issue that is mentioned several times elsewhere (pp. 43 and 180): the different roles staff members have to take up in order to make up a whole team that will adequately meet the needs of the clients. The issue itself is central to the functioning of the establishment, and supervision must be prepared to engage with it; but this is a very difficult area, the one most fraught with possibilities for manipulation, and the one where trust and confidentiality face their sorest tests. The problem is very simple indeed: bitching. More than that, staff members have been known to report their supervisor's remarks outside the session in support of some personal vendetta, which can cause untold problems.

It may seem cynical that my initial remarks about staff roles focus on the destructive possibilities implicit in discussing them, but this is one of those situations where the supervisor has to be aware of the 'worst possible outcomes' factor. If this is in the back of your mind all the time, then it will help you keep to the task when the matter comes up. Whereas in the other topics we have examined the overall assumption (even in looking at incidents) has been that the staff member's account of the situation is at least adequately professional, the same cannot necessarily be assumed in relation to staff roles. This is not because staff are liars, fabricators, or fantasizers, but because anything that involves one personally is the most difficult thing to see clearly. The problem is compounded by the fact that the supervisor is also part of the same system, and therefore her own view is likely to be pretty unreliable as well.

So instead of providing the list of stimulus questions, as in the previous sections, let us look at some of the levels at which these matters of staff role may be raised and discussed.

(1) The first is the *managerial dimension*. If a staff member complains about the stereotyping of male and female roles in the establishment, or of never having the opportunity to try something he thinks he would be good at, then the first possibility to consider is whether the structure of the unit provides space for change or not.

It is possible, for example, that there is a policy decision that the models of male and female roles presented to the residents should be as conventional as possible (because when the clients are out of step with the rest of society on so many other counts, it is not fair to burden them with any more forms of deviation). If that is the case, however debatable the idea, then it is clear that some areas of work will be denied to the women on the staff; and equally they will get lumbered with some other, usually less attractive areas. If they complain about this, it is a management question as to whether you change the policy and hence the structure in order to provide the space for the women (and the men) to change roles, or whether you explain the logic of the present position and let them get on with it. If it is a matter for management action, then the Head of Home must be careful not to be badgered into changing it simply by the forcefulness of one staff member in supervision. There are other channels for initiating change (e.g. the staff meeting) and they should be seen to be used. Supevision should not become a back-door lobbying procedure

(2) There is the issue of the complementarity and conflict of roles in the informal working of the staff group. For example, the supervisor wants the staff member to broaden his working base from his usual disciplinarian style. But, he complains, the others will not let him change. They like him to be the hard man so that they can get on with being close and warm towards the clients. He has to take all the nasty bits. This is a very difficult

situation to resolve, because in the staff member's account there are a number of possibilities:

- He may be right; the resistance comes from outside.
- He may be right, as above, but the problem is compounded by the fact that he cannot tolerate as much disorder as his colleagues can.
- He may be projecting on to his colleagues the justification for his behaviour, which is principally accounted for by his own rigidity.
- He may resent their attitude towards the clients, which he sees as soft, namby-pamby, or even fearful.
- There may be a combination of any of these factors that results in a collusion which is not fully understood by anyone in the situation.

Additionally, the supervisor may be concerned about the extent to which any attempt to change the staff member's role will destabilize the group as a whole. She may also not be clear in her own mind about where she stands on the control–permissiveness issue; and it may even be the case that the allocation of roles within the staff team has grown up because of a lack of clear leadership.

In this case there is a need to get permission from the staff member to go public with the issue, raising it in group supervision if possible. If change is required from two parties, both the individual and his group, this cannot effectively be achieved through one-to-one work alone. The supervisor in her turn needs to look at her own part in it all, with her own supervisor.

Dysfunctional complementary roles are a harder problem to handle than conflict and disagreements, because they often go unrecognized until there is a crisis.

(3) A third dimension is that what is going on in the staff room is an unrecognized reflection, usually a distorted one, of what is going on in the resident group. Always check to find out if there are parallels, analogues, or mirror-images between the two groups. The simplest approach to this is

to focus on whether changes in one group are followed a little later by changes in the other. Then there is the work to be done to get this recognized by the staff, who like most people would rather regard themselves as responsible for their own feelings and destinies.

(4) But the staff are individual human beings as well. Like everyone else they have their personal preferences regarding other people; and it is not unknown for such feelings to become attached to professional issues, quite accidentally. They have every right to love or hate each other.

(5) What is presented as a problem of role may be a matter of personal survival. For example, a member of staff may have carved out a nice little niche for herself, always bustling around and looking after the physical needs of the residents, whilst complaining that she never has any time to talk to them about their problems. She would be scared stiff if she were ever asked to do any counselling; but as long as she grumbles she is able to say, 'I'm just as professional as you are, or I would be if I had the chance.'

Since most human relationships are over-determined (i.e. the result of several causes working together and amplifying each other) it is likely that in any given circumstance more than one of these dimensions will apply. In terms of 'solutions', supervision is not very effective; and it is here that one can be thankful that supervision is not the only contribution one makes to work in the establishment!

Where supervision can contribute however, is in the essential task of helping each staff member to examine her own perceptions and to entertain the possibility that they may be distorted by elements of fantasy. The crude rule of thumb is to pretend that you know nothing about the situation except what the staff member brings with her into the session; and then work with her on looking at what she is saying about herself, and hence about her part and contribution to the whole.

The internal politics of the staff group often generate more intense feeling and discussion than even the activities of the clients. Those involved take it for granted, and tend to seek explanations in terms of individual personalities, ambitions, or perhaps cliques. My own belief is that, just as in Freud's view dreams are the royal road to the unconscious, so staff dynamics are the royal road to understanding the hidden life of a residential establishment. This alone is sufficient reason to take them seriously in supervision, and to try to cultivate a climate in which staff members are capable of standing back from their personal involvement and investment to ask, 'What is really going on here, and what can I learn from it about the establishment at large?'

Both the staff and the resident groups are influenced not only by things happening inside the home, but also by what happens outside it. Therefore the behaviour of neither staff nor residents is an infallible guide to the whole, on its own. What is reliable is the existence of common themes in the two groups, often acted out in different ways. The staff group is often the one to demonstrate the theme more clearly, because the group tends to be more articulate. But it needs to be checked out in the resident group as well. The correspondence between the manifestations of the theme is by no means always direct. The example most often quoted is where the authoritarian structure of an establishment at a staff level is mimicked in a distorted form in bullying and exploitation among the residents. (See, for example, Polsky 1965; Wills 1971.) In that case, the parallel seems clear; but there are occasions when the same problem is treated in diametrically opposed ways in the two groups. Isolating the common themes, and working out what they are, is therefore rather like listening to a complex piece of music and trying to disentangle the variations that have been woven together. Sometimes a theme is repeated displaced in key, sometimes displaced in time, sometimes even reversed in sequence or pitch – but it remains the same theme. The sophisticated residential practitioner finds himself doing this exercise of disentanglement intuitively; but supervision is one of the opportunities for developing the skill – rather like a music student who hears the music, or even plays it, and then sits down with a teacher and the score in front of him and learns to recognize the patterns in it.

This section has touched on some fairly complex and demanding issues: from the practicalities of survival as a supervisor discussing staff rules, to the rarefied atmosphere of what amounts to the psychoanalysis of communal life (de Board 1978). This reflects what happens when the topic of staff roles comes up. You find yourself continually moving up and down the scale, from intellectual puzzling about what it means, to feeling guilty because it all seems like an adverse comment on your management skills, to watching your own back in how to phrase a point, to trying to be diplomatic, to confrontation.

You can never get it all right all the time, so take a cautious guideline to begin with; think, 'How can I handle this in such a way as to avoid making the situation *worse*, in the relatively long term?' Once you have learned to answer this question effectively, much of the rest will be added without your realizing it.

### THEORY

Supervision is not a tutorial, and the kind of supervision discussed here is not the same as study supervision on a training course. None the less, discussion of theoretical models does come up as part of supervision, and so some observations on the subject need to be made.

(1) Assuming that there is a reason for the way everything is done within the home, a staff member needs to understand that reason sufficiently clearly to be able to carry through the policy without being tempted to change it for the sake of personal convenience or some delusion of knowing a 'better way'. This hardly qualifies as 'theory', you may think, but theory is what it is. (This goes back to the section on routines, p. 95 ff.) This is not meant to stifle honest disagreement and discussion as to the best way of

handling things, but it is meant to ensure that staff are clear about the reasons for practice as it is, and therefore aware of the possible consequences of varying it. Without this understanding, they become automatons, once again 'only obeying orders' – and usually unnecessarily rigid about it; or they become random free agents who are unable to provide the continuity and consistency of care that clients have a right to expect.

(2) There are also many situations in which the staff member has great scope for choice in his course of action, situations where there are no set rules. When one girl complains that another girl has got her knickers on, he may say, 'Tough', and forget the matter; he may pursue the matter; he may propose an *ad hoc* bit of policy for knicker-control; he may confront the supposed culprit; he may refer the girl to a female member of staff; he may back off suspecting the prelude to a sexually compromising situation; or he may do any one of many other things. Whether what he does – at the level of a recipe or of a well-thought-out response – contributes to or hinders the progress of the girls in the establishment will depend on whether he has some theoretical perspective in his head to refer to. The Head of Home cannot lay down rules for every possible eventuality, but the variability of individual staff decisions can confuse policy enormously, unless they share some kind of theoretical perspective and value-base.

The selection of theory to be taught is not made in order that it can be 'applied' or imposed on experience. Make a task analysis of what staff do, put this in the context of what the establishment tries to do, and the theory will be there. You just have to recognize it and pass it on. It will *probably* include some ideas about human growth and development, some about the aims of residential social work, some about group processes, some about the nature of disturbance in individuals and families, and so on. Undertaking this exercise of uncovering implicit and inarticulate theories may reveal that their justification is not always clear or that they are not shared by everyone. In that case, they need to be talked through with your supervisor, or a training officer, or a college tutor, or anyone else who just might know, backed up by some reading to check them out.

The place of theoretical teaching in supervision is therefore limited, but still important. In undertaking it, however, the following factors need to be borne in mind.

First, many residential practitioners are suspicious of theory. They see it as bearing little relation to the confused, wearing, and sometimes sordid reality of residential life in an over-stretched local authority establishment with insufficient and untrained staff, and a continual pressure to take an admission – however inappropriately placed – whenever there is a bed vacant. But to ignore theory altogether is not only to deprive self and staff of a possible resource, it is also phoney.

Everybody works on the basis of theories. Everyday working theories shade into fantasies and prejudices, but they are still theories. So we are not talking about no-theory versus theory in residential work, but about the use of formal theories as opposed to 'inarticulate' theories – ideas in people's heads that influence their actions but which they never spell out.

Second, the primary requirement of a theory is that it should be *useful*. This comes even before the requirement that it should be accurate. Theories, whether inarticulate or well worked out and backed by plenty of evidence, are primarily ways of organizing experience and data. They are containers for it, which enable it to be drawn upon, applied to different situations, used, learned from, and built on. The test of a good theory is therefore whether it enables us to make use of experience.

Third, the next requirement of a theory is that it should do justice to our experience, and be accurate. However, there are occasions when people continue to work on the basis of theories that they know to be inaccurate, because the accurate ones are too complicated to handle. At a 'respectable' level, for example, surveyors still work *as if* the sun went round the earth. Engineers on the whole work as if Einstein had never been born. Astronomers, on the other hand, could not possibly work on either of these bases.

But there is also a problem about what constitutes 'accuracy' on the part of a theory. We may draw narrow boundaries around the issue under discussion so that the theory can deal with it, perhaps at the cost of excluding very important factors. So, for example, we tend to look at the behaviour of a person as if it were the product of individual personality and individual pathology. Sometimes, for all practical purposes, this works; but an accurate account of the person's behaviour will have to take into account the peer group, the family, the cultural background, and perhaps the economic state of the country. However, because that gets too unwieldy, we plump for theories that, perhaps accurate enough within their own sphere of competence, may do gross injustice to the evidence of the whole.

Fourth, particularly in the social 'sciences', there are many competing theories to account for the same phenomena. All of them may be able to explain things adequately in the end, so how do you choose between them?

Fifth, theories explain things, but they do not explain them away. One of Freud's favourite sayings was borrowed from his one-time teacher, Charcot: 'La théorie est bonne, mais ça n'empêche pas d'exister.' This translates roughly as: 'The theory is fine, but it doesn't make it go away.' We often fall into this trap of believing that once we have explained something, or labelled it, we have somehow gained power over it – as if all a doctor had to do was diagnose a disease correctly, whereupon it would disappear without having to treat it!

Sixth, we choose theories that are on the whole consistent with our other ways of looking at things, so that they will coexist inside our heads without too much friction. This naturally has implications for new theories that we adopt, because either they have to coexist with what we already believe, or we have to put theories about different things in watertight compartments that do not touch each other, or we have to face re-evaluating everything we believe in order to accommodate a new idea.

All the above points make it clear that theoretical considerations are far from sterile academic issues. Correspondingly, teaching theory in supervision can be easy or difficult. It is easy when the staff member has become aware of a need for a framework to handle otherwise elusive or baffling experience. It is difficult when you seem to be talking to a brick wall, when all you encounter is obtuseness, apparent stupidity, and inability to understand or retain even the simplest formulations. It can be even more difficult when you see that the ideas appeal greatly, but the staff member cannot allow herself to accept them: 'If I believed that, I'd have to give up this work', or 'If that's true, I've been doing it wrong all these years!' (See Chapter 11, 'Learning and Change'.)

Since every statement a person makes has some theoretical content – and, even more powerful, some statement of value – it is important to build up a picture of what your staff member believes *now*. Generally speaking, this can be achieved through concentrated listening and reflection afterwards, but there are occasions when devices like the Repertory Grid prove useful. (See Kelly 1955; Bannister and Fransella 1980.) The theoretical perspective put forward by the supervisor is generally competing with the resident theory in the marketplace of the staff member's mind, and so it is important to know the competition. Further, many theories are inseparable from strongly held values, and these are even harder to change. We have all had the sensation of feeling that 'there's just nothing I can do', when we seem to be speaking a different language from either a resident or a staff member. It is necessary to be clear in your mind just what language she is speaking.

There are some of us who project such an air of dogmatic certainty about what we believe (in terms of both value and theoretical ideas) that we brook no contradiction. Sometimes this is a great leadership quality; sometimes it is the tip of the iceberg of insensitive boorishness. There are occasions when it is appropriate to 'sell' a particular idea in supervision; but since the crucial test is whether ideas are put into practice outside the supervision session, these occasions are fewer than the convinced believer might wish to accept. There is no point in procuring assent to dogmatic propositions, if all the staff member is going to do is heave a sigh of relief on leaving the session and go back to thinking and behaving just as she did before.

The introduction of theoretical perspectives does not have to be highly academic. There is much value in simple analogies, for example. To draw attention to the similarities between one thing and another is to focus on important strands or processes, and to highlight them by showing how they work in a different context. Sometimes analogies are clichés – 'It's like beating your head against a brick wall, talking to him' – but they can still make communication more vivid even when they do not add anything else. On occasion you may wish to contest them:

> 'It seems to me not so much like banging your head against a brick wall as punching a foam cushion. When you've still got your fist there, you seem to have made some impression, but as soon as you take it away, the cushion is exactly the same as it was before.'

If this analogy is accepted as more accurate, you can then go on to raise the question about what it is in Billy's view of the world that leads him to adapt under pressure, but to revert when the pressure is removed. In fact, this kind of analogy is probably more direct use in supervision than a long spiel about Becker on situational adjustment and committed change (Becker 1970).

Words are not always the best way of communicating theory. Pictures and diagrams can be considerably more vivid. As every teacher knows, even very abstract ideas stick in the mind all the better for being laid out in such a way to illuminate the relationship of ideas to each other. *Draw* things at every available opportunity; write down key words; use symbols or matchstick figures. The activity helps to focus the discussion; there is something for the staff member to take away and to meditate upon; and, bearing in mind that the test of theory is its usefulness, in the working situation it is easier to call to mind a graphic image than a string of words.

Similarly, the written word has its place. Make a practice of clipping out articles from the social work press and other sources, and file them, so that they can be passed on when a topic comes up that they might illuminate. Make a note of books, either in a notebook or on a card index, including full details for ordering from a bookshop or library (author, title, place of publication, publisher, and date; see the References list of this book for examples), and the library classification code if the book was borrowed from a library. Check the local libraries to see what other books they have in the field, and find out what is held in the agency library. Residential staff are not great readers of their professional literature; but if you can point them specifically to a text that will say something about an issue which already concerns them, they are likely to respond. Always follow this up; ask at the next session what the staff member thought of the article or book, and tie it back to practice as much as possible.

## FACTS

If theories are the underpinnings of practice, facts in social work often set out the limits of the space within which one works. When we believe theories, we tend to accord them the status of facts, and to teach them as if there were no question about them. The matron (she still thinks of herself as that) of a nursery rebuked a member of her staff for picking up a crying child, telling her that 'picking up children when they cry spoils them'. She believed that as a *fact*: but it is no more than a theory, and a discredited one at that. There are very few facts as such in social work.

Facts set out the limits of practice, because those facts that may be treated as such are often of the legal and regulatory variety, or concern information about the environment that conditions the way in which one can go about doing the job:

- So-called voluntary admission to care is covered in section 2 of the Child Care Act 1980.
- The fire regulations demand that this door be kept closed.
- The doctor's telephone number is . . .
- The cans of beans are on the top shelf on the right.

A lot of induction training is concerned with facts, and apart from some more complex items of information – such as legal provisions – they are not often seen as important for supervision. Nevertheless there are a few points worth making about them:

- What facts do your staff need to know?
- Do all staff need to know the same things?
- What do they need to remember, and what do they need to know how to find out when they need it?
- For example, how much medical knowledge ought a care assistant to have?

(This is one of those cases where believing something to be true when it isn't is more dangerous than not knowing anything about it at all; the limits of knowledge are important, too). On the whole, supervision is not the place to pass on facts, because it can be done more effectively and efficiently in groups, but it may well be the place to check that people really do know them. A snap 'test' – if it is fully understood that there is no condemnation in not knowing the answer, but there is in guessing – does have its place in supervision.

Facts relate to constraints and resources, and so control of information is ultimately a political matter, both in the selection of the facts available and in their interpretation. In order to delegate, you must ensure that there are some things that staff do know. This tends to be overlooked, and so it is worth including in the contract. It need not take up much time, but it can avoid a lot of problems. Supervisors, in both field and residential settings, frequently wail when things have gone wrong: 'But he ought to have known *that*! After all, he's got his CQSW (or CSS)!' Such assumptions cannot be made; they need to be checked all the time.

It is pretty tough on the staff member if all you do is test her and give her no opportunity to learn. Despite our experience of schooling, where enormous effort went into learning meaningless facts, a deficiency of knowledge is relatively easy to rectify – easier than the development of skills or a change in values. Relevance is the key; if staff can see the application of what they have to learn, they will learn it with little trouble and effort. For 'topping-up' purposes, discussion in supervision easily demonstrates relevance. The next step is to have material to hand that the staff member can use outside the session to learn the facts. She may need only to read it once or twice so that she knows what is in it, as long as she also knows where it is to refer to when required.

Make a habit of collecting such useful information, and file it systematically so that there is a resources bank for staff to use when they need to. Not everyone needs to know the same things in the same detail, so select and digest material for them (as long as the whole thing is also available). If several staff plead ignorance, this is one case where one can legitimately put material from supervision sessions together, and ask the training section or some other resource to come in and give some input at the staff meeting.

Don't overlook the humble notice-board. As long as it is kept clear of out-of-date rubbish, and staff are encouraged to look at it (how long do you spend gazing at it in the office while you are waiting for the phone to be answered at the other end?), it can be a very effective means of getting information over. (Just one point: don't put up pamphlets that need to be turned over, hanging on a string; they do not get read. Keep it simple and vivid.)

# Part Three

# 9 Introducing Supervision

Although gaining ground rapidly, supervision is still compara-
tively rare in group-care establishments. Sometimes its introduction is easy, because staff are already aware – perhaps
through experience of study supervison on in-service or CSS
programmes – of the benefits to be derived from it. But since
residential and day-care work has never had the tradition of
professional supervision enjoyed by fieldwork, its introduction
can be experienced as threatening. New entrants to the work
do not know what to expect, and old hands have developed
their own survival techniques that enable them to get by
apparently satisfactorily. For the latter group in particular, the
introduction of supervision may be seen as a vote of no
confidence in the work they have been doing for all these
years. Furthermore, it is time-consuming, and entails a
number of consequential changes in the procedures and the
organization of the establishment.

So there are a number of obstacles to be overcome in its
introduction; but supervision programmes rely for their
success on the co-operation of all concerned, and so the
obstacles cannot simply be steamrollered away by high-
handed managerial action. Instead, the issues they raise need
to be taken seriously; it is the contention of this chapter that
examining them not only helps to overcome them, but can also
teach everyone concerned a number of interesting things
about the life of the establishment.

Not only the potential supervisees may object, of course.
Future supervisors may also have their doubts, and these need
to be answered if the new idea is to take root and flourish.

MANAGING INNOVATION

The introduction of supervision is just one case of an innovation in a group-care establishment. The following remarks are intended to be no more than simplified pointers to what may be going on.

## The 'natural state' of the system

A group-care establishment, like any other system, has a natural state to which it tends to return when it is at rest. There may be a lot going on, but it is all in the interests of keeping the situation 'ticking over' in its natural state. There will be built-in control mechanisms, which ensure that when the natural balance is disturbed the system makes every effort to restore it. (In the jargon, this is known as 'homeostasis'; see Waddington 1977; Watzlawick, Weakland, and Fisch 1973.)

Our bodies have a natural working temperature, for example. When we are too hot, we sweat in an effort to lower the temperature; when too cold, we get goose-pimples and shiver, trying to raise it. If the balance is disturbed too much, we die. Most of the time we do not even notice the temperature changes, because the balancing mechanism works so efficiently.

In the same way as our attention is drawn to our body temperature only when we encounter variations from it, attention is mainly drawn to the state of our establishment when we are trying to get it back on an 'even keel' – back to its natural state. Paradoxically, then, we find out what that natural state is only when it is threatened or changed – by an innovation, for example.

So by watching what happens when we try to change things, we might discover evidence about what is normally going on to which we would not otherwise have access. This can be of value in terms of the overall development programme of the unit, as well as in supervision itself. In this context, it is important to realize that what goes on in the unit as a whole may be very different from the intentions and ideas of any of the individuals who go to make up the staff or client groups.

## Enthusiasm

If a change is greeted with enthusiasm, then this means that it fits in with the culture and natural tendency of the establishment. The likelihood of this is a matter of timing, among other variables; unless there is a great deal of active discontent with the way things are at present, people generally do not want to take on board too many changes at the same time.

## Resistance

Resistance generally indicates that you are either deliberately or unintentionally changing an aspect of the culture that is fairly important to those involved. Resistance is not simply bloody-mindedness; it is the natural response of a self-regulating system to any attempt to change it. The effect is similar to that of trying to swim against the tide or of rolling a boulder uphill. Once the effort to create the change slackens a little, the natural state of the system will reassert itself. Real headway will be made, not by increasing the effort put into this particular change, but if possible by altering the circumstances within which the change will operate – wait until the tide changes, or flatten the hill. (See Chapter 3, 'Preparing the Ground', for some ideas in this area.)

It may not be the innovation itself that is being resisted, but one of its side-effects. For example, if you decide to practise supervision during change-over periods, and this meets with objections, it may not be the supervision itself that is the problem so much as that staff are used to using change-over to catch up on their own internal gossip. They may not feel able to say this, because change-over time is not intended for that in any case. So the objection becomes focused on the supervision programme itself.

Resistances can be of three major kinds:

- *Realistic*. There are occasions when ideas are actually wrong for the unit and you should always assume that there is good reason for objections and resistance until proven otherwise.
- *Fantasy* – based on a misunderstanding of what the innovation is about. Innovation in the form of the introduction of supervision, for example, may be seen as a vote of no confidence in what staff are doing at the moment and as a means of increasing control over them. Fantasies can be proved to be correct, and they are more difficult to meet than realistic objections.
- *Defensive* – in which a fantasy is strengthened by an additional sense of threat. This is the hardest kind of resistance to overcome, and yet the kind that says most about the hidden culture of the establishment. (See Menzies's famous case-study of nursing, 1967.)

**Passive acceptance**

At least you know where you stand when resistance is out in the open. The problem with passive acceptance is that it can mean any number of things:

- *Resistance + fear*. Possibly the staff would like to object, but they are so scared that they dare not. So they simply grumble about the change but apparently go along with it.
- *Irrelevance*. This does not mean that the change is not important, but simply that at this time it is not seen by staff as touching on any of their vested interests.

Will the change stick? Some changes can be made with no fuss; but in many cases of passive acceptance you can find that there is a lack of motivation to make them work. Hence when any difficulties arise the new ideas are quietly dropped.

**Varied responses**

Some people like innovation, some people don't, and some are just not bothered. This is one of the most likely patterns, and it indicates the existence of sub-groupings of some kind within the staff team. (There is just a possibility that everyone is reacting purely as an individual, but if this is the case, then you have problems anyway!) Each sub-group has to be approached on a different basis; and if they are in conflict, there is the difficulty that what will please one will offend the others. However, each sub-group says something about the overall character of the establishment, and it may be that each represents in greater measure than normal a set of values or feelings that to some extent belong to everyone – including the innovator.

The central lesson is to listen to what each of the responses is saying about the whole social system, and to respond to that. This may be a complicated exercise, and often it does not yield rapid results, but it puts any kind of innovation on a much firmer footing. You really need your own supervisor or a consultant to help to do this.

## SOME CONCRETE OBJECTIONS

In the light of the above general remarks, some of the specific objections commonly raised against the introduction of supervision are discussed briefly below.

### 'There's no time'

There are two main reasons for putting forward this idea. The first is that there is too much for the supervisor to do (it is usually the supervisor who is short of time, rather than the more junior staff). But how much of the potential supervisor's time is spent overseeing junior staff and making minor decisions, because they cannot be delegated because the staff are not capable of making them because they have not had the benefit of supervision? The deputy superintendent of one assessment centre spends at least half his time in staff supervision; *because* he does so he has more time than before to spend with the children. The argument is of the same order as 'I can't afford to insulate my home because my fuel bills are so high.'

The second version of 'there's no time' is slightly different. The potential supervisor feels that she gets little enough time with the clients as it is; and she did come into the work to work with them after all. The answer to this is rather harsh. Having less direct client contact is part of the price of the greater authority that goes with a senior position. If she cannot sort out her priorities, she is getting her personal job satisfaction at the cost of the overall well-being of the clients, and she ought to reconsider whether she is in the right job. The primary duty of senior staff is to create the space within which clients can be cared for and worked with. They may have the spare time to spend with them, or they may make it because it is important for other reasons (such as not being a threatening figure isolated in an office, or because they need that personal contact in order to keep going); but they are failing if they are not creating that working space. However, it just may happen that, in the light of the previous paragraph, the supervisor ends up with more time to spend with clients, rather than less.

### 'I've tried it and it doesn't work'

Two questions arise when this object is made. First, exactly what was tried? I'd like to suggest, very humbly, that you read the rest of this book before declaring that you have tried it. How long was it 'tried' for (and what counts as it 'not working')? Supervision is not an instant panacea, and it may well take some time before its benefits become apparent. In fact, there is a suggestion from some practitioners that when it is introduced things get worse before they get better. (See Chapter 6, 'The Supervision Session'.) Before dismissing it, make sure that it is not being condemned for failing to do something it never set out to do in the first place; see Chapter 1, 'Aims and Objectives of Supervision'.

From the supervisor's point of view, the above are the two most common 'presenting objections'. But they often stand for more powerful kinds of resistance that are rarely voiced; one of these is structural (even political), and the other personal.

### 'It threatens our present way of working'

Ironically, I have encountered this objection several times masked by the 'I've tried it . . . ' story. It is ironic because the excuse is that supervision is too weak, and the real resistance comes from the fantasy that it is too powerful. There is a belief that it undermines the authority of the senior staff; that it makes it impossible to give a direct order; that everything has to be delegated; that it removes the possibility of keeping anything confidential; and that it leads junior staff to get above themselves. All of these may be potentially true, but such fears are rarely realized. They are the same fears as those underlying resistance to staff meetings, which have largely been conquered in most establishments. Professional supervision is indeed incompatible with several approaches to management and leadership, and most seriously it is a threat to the 'mushroom' model of management – keep them in the dark and cover them with muck from time to time. It is also a threat to benevolent paternalism, which is more common, and not quite as destructive in the short term.

But for many staff, it is much more a matter of rocking a pretty good boat – a reluctance to introduce something with unknown outcomes that might prove to cause more problems than it solves. This feeling needs to be taken seriously, but it does imply a degree of complacency, and perhaps a potential inability to adapt to changing circumstances. The most successful species in the history of the Earth was the dinosaur!

### 'I'd be embarrassed'

This is the second unspoken objection: the personal one. If the potential supervisor has been getting along very well up to now on the basis of occasional informal chats when the opportunity has presented itself, if relationships with staff are easy-going and spontaneous, and if he is not confident of his abilities in this field, then to formalize the process of supervision is to introduce an element of self-consciousness, which it is all too easy for staff to misunderstand.

If the introduction of professional supervision is going to upset relationships as feared, then it suggests that the comfortable culture that seems to exist is in fact fragile, and perhaps even phoney. The characteristic of a truly strong, easy-going relationship in an establishment is that it has *redundancy* (a term that originated in linguistics; if you are of a psychoanalytic turn of mind, you could say the relationship was 'over-determined'). Redundancy means that there are a number of factors all having similar effects in contributing to the same end, like the strands that make up a rope. The relationship does not take on its present form merely because of informality, for example; there are other features, such as mutual respect, trust, and a shared history, that make it what it is. In not considering those other features of the relationship with staff you may well be underestimating yourself and the strength of what has been built up in the staff group. The introduction of professional supervision may strain some elements of the relationship for a short while, but the investment is 90 per cent certain to start paying off well before the funds of goodwill are overdrawn.

Lack of confidence about supervising may not be such a drawback, either. Don't be afraid of it. Share it. If it is shared, this new innovation can turn into a joint experiment, which will encourage staff to commit themselves to making it work. Trying to cover up a lack of confidence, on the other hand, may well lead staff to feel that supervision is something that is to be done *to* them; this in turn leads to resentment and to efforts to pick holes in the supervisor's technique and competence. After a while the spontaneity of the relationship will return, but this time it will also embrace the acceptance of the roles of supervisor and supervisee.

A further cause of embarrassment, however, is the extent to which engaging in supervision may expose to others the supervisor's prejudices and values, skills and weaknesses. The likelihood is that these are exposed already through the normal working situation, despite any efforts to conceal them! But if this is a real anxiety, then discussion with your own supervisor is necessary.

If there is one message in all this for those who decide to start supervision, it is that it is important to see a supervision programme as a co-operative enterprise, in which both parties are learners, and in which mistakes can be admitted and laughed at. The only sure recipe for disaster is to over-compensate for your own uncertainty by setting out in an arrogant and pompous way that puts down the staff member. I know – I did it that way first!

STAFF RELUCTANCE

Let us now turn to some aspects of the resistance that may be encountered from the staff side. Perhaps the commonest way of 'selling' supervision to staff is as a means of support, and this is quite a good strategy. But don't be tempted to believe that staff have no other means of support. Supervision is entering a market in which there are already other established products. Staff already get support from their peers; for each hour spent in formal supervision sessions or staff meetings, far more is likely to be spent in informal chats between staff, while sorting out the laundry, or drinking coffee, or over a pint off-duty. I would be the last to decry the usefulness of these sessions; many establishments could not operate without the support offered to frustrated and despairing young members of staff by a well-established mother- or father-figure within the staff group. The absence of such a figure often contributes to the coldness and emptiness that are almost tangible in the atmosphere of some otherwise admirable units. Yet such support may meet the felt needs of the staff, while not meeting the overall development needs of the work in the establishment.

Informal support, from peers or anyone else,

(1) is unaccountable, in the sense that it is not 'plugged in' to the task of the establishment;
(2) is based on friendship rather than on professional role relationships;

(3) has no set boundaries that enable people to be pushed to learn;
(4) may be based on fantasies and gossip, with no effort to check out the reality;
(5) may contribute to the setting up of a staff subculture based on survival needs rather than on professional concerns;
(6) may, following from the above, contribute to the labelling of clients, and 'fixing' them in roles they cannot escape from.

Apart from (5) and (6), none of the above features are 'bad'; it is just that they limit what can be achieved to the 'warm bath', and hence are no substitute for a proper supervision programme. Indeed, it can be argued that the stronger the informal support network in an establishment, the greater is the need for a supervision programme.

The rule is to harness the informal system where it is complementary to the formal one, and to remove its power source where it is opposed. To do the latter means a thorough examination of the culture of the establishment, to identify where the energy is coming from. This is never easy, and the results usually contain some uncomfortable material for the senior staff; but this material has to be faced and worked through if supervision (or any other innovation) is not to run into a brick wall.

THE POINT IS TO CHANGE IT (MARX)

The quotation runs: 'The philosophers have only interpreted the world: the point is to change it.' That might be said about the preceding remarks, but what do you actually *do* to overcome any resistances?

(1) Take them seriously. Don't try to ride roughshod over them. Successful supervision programmes depend on the co-operation of staff, and you will not get that if there is an undercurrent of resentment all the time.
(2) If there are other changes that have to be made first, then make them. Sometimes this can go hand in hand with the

introduction of supervision, but it is important that enough is seen to be done to make staff aware that the changes are for real and not merely cosmetic. (There is a problem here if the changes that staff want are in fact against good professional practice.)

(3) Work through the informal leaders within the staff – the opinion-formers. Win them over, and others will follow. This may sound devious, but I'm not suggesting that you suborn, blackmail, or strong-arm them, merely that you make use of the informal networks that already exist.

(4) Emphasize the beneficial consequences of the change – not only for the staff but also for the clients. Despite any impression I may have given, the vast majority of staff are very much concerned for the well-being of clients. But don't fudge any problems that may be anticipated; staff will then feel they have been conned, and not only this innovation but subsequent ones will founder because you are not seen as trustworthy.

(5) If at all possible, let people see the change in action, by visiting somewhere where it is established practice and talking to people already working with it. This place ought to be as like your own as possible; otherwise there will be objections based on 'It's all very well for them, but we can't do it here because . . .'

(6) Without being obstinate, demonstrate commitment and enthusiam for the idea. If staff think you are just going through the motions, they are not likely to want to follow.

(7) At all times and all stages, *consult* others. It may be time-consuming and sometimes frustrating, but it is the only way.

CONCLUSION

The introduction of supervision into an established residential or day-care unit is not easy – not necessarily because of anyone's conscious obstruction, but because nothing happens in isolation in such establishments. After they have been in existence for a while without major changes (in the client group, staff, domestic and other support, and task), establishments find their own level of functioning, which is determined by a host of factors, with a high degree of redundancy. Any attempt to change one element of the whole, without taking others into account, is pretty well doomed to failure; *plus ça change, plus c'est la même chose*. (See Watzlawick, Weakland and Fisch on 'first-order change', 1973.)

The introduction of professional supervision is not simply the introduction of a technique. It marks a slight change of direction in the working of an establishment. It makes little sense unless it is accompanied by a devolution of authority to individual staff members. It fits very well with the introduction of a key-worker system. It points towards the replacement of a culture based on clear structural rules by one that allows for more discretion and more initiative, and that expects more professionalism. Like any change, it is costly. Staff can no longer rely on simply working by the book, regardless of individual circumstances. They are less likely to have the security of 'just obeying orders'. Senior staff have to cope with anxiety about juniors doing things for which seniors are accountable but without having direct control over them.

Such changes are accompanied by testing-out on the part of the staff. Although it is to be hoped that the basic dependable structure of the establishment will not be affected adversely, problems are bound to arise and these may cause questions to be asked by the agency management. Residents are just as sensitive as anyone else to changes in their living environment (and rightly so – they are the ones who actually *live* there) and they may well put in their pennyworth. One might even go so far as to say that *unless* there are some of these problems supervision is not being done properly.

So, is it worth it? If this chapter has been gloomy and has seemed to present a far-fetched picture of resistance, distrust, and unforeseen disruption, that is because I have needed to show the cost of supervision clearly. It is not a gimmick that can be picked up for a while and then dropped again when it becomes inconvenient. It requires commitment, investment, and a degree of risk.

# 10　The Supervisory Relationship

The supervisor is not some paragon of virtue, but a normal social worker (if such an animal exists). However, there are skills and qualities that contribute to the effectiveness of supervision, as far as we can tell, and many of these can be developed by practice and a little theory to leaven the lump.

## On being good enough

We owe to Winnicott the formulation of the expression 'good-enough mother' (Winnicott 1971). It is remarkably reassuring, because it conveys that while it may be impossible to be perfect most people can manage to be satisfactory in a role for all practical purposes. The same applies to the supervisor. If, in what follows, I seem to be pointing in the direction of a perfect identikit supervisor, it is worth bearing in mind that that perfection does not exist.

### SUPERVISION AND COUNSELLING

Supervision is not the same thing as counselling, primarily because counselling is undertaken for the benefit of the client – who corresponds to the supervisee – and supervision is undertaken for the benefit of the residents, not primarily for the supervisee. I am not really interested in the feelings or problems of the staff member himself, except in so far as he needs to be able to contain or resolve them in such a way as to free him to work effectively with the residents. Having said that, there are obvious parallels between a supervision session and a counselling session, and they repay a certain amount of examination.

First, we have two people sitting down deliberately to talk about something, in a session that is as far as possible screened from interruptions and distractions. It is a working session rather than a social chit-chat, and the effectiveness of the session is to be assessed by what happens outside it, rather than within it.

Second, it can work effectively only if the recipient of the help offered (the client or the supervisee) is able and prepared to tell the truth about the issues under discussion. This naturally entails the existence of a degree of trust between the participants. Trust in this context is not to be assessed as a vague sense of emotional security but as a preparedness to tell the truth – almost the whole truth – and to work at the outcomes. It is salutary to note that while the counsellor or supervisor can create the conditions (both inside and outside the session) for trust, the person who is doing the trusting is the client or supervisee, and this cannot be legislated for.

Third, both counselling and supervision are quite powerful activities, with potential to hinder as well as to help. (For a summary of research on the hindering as well as helping capacities of counselling, see Truax and Carkhuff 1967.) Counselling can easily become destructive rather than con-structive. Supervision is slightly different, but only because it is not so dependent on the relationship between the supervisor and the staff member. A poor relationship can cut down the benefit derived from supervision, but it is not as likely to militate against an overall outcome on the credit side as might be the case with a poor counselling relationship. Supervision is merely one component of the management of staff practice which has a fairly high degree of redundancy. There are the policies, procedures, and routines of the establishment; there are managerial directives; there is back-up from other staff. All of these together (if they are working together) may reinforce the messages of supervision.

However, the parallels are sufficiently close to make it worth while to devote some space to the classic threefold qualities of the counsellor, and to recommend that they be adopted as principles in supervision. These three qualities are *empathy*, *warmth*, and *genuineness* (Truax and Carkhuff 1967).

## EMPATHY

Empathy comes first, because there is a sense in which the other two qualities are means towards being able to sustain it. Empathy is *the ability to see the world from the other person's point of view*, also expressed as the ability to put oneself in someone else's shoes and to feel where they pinch. This is an extension of the general injunction that has already been emphasized: to start from where the staff member *is* rather than from where you feel that he ought to be. But there is more. Empathy requires, in practical terms, that you listen to what the other person is saying in such a way as to share their world or their experience.

It is as if the supervisor (or counsellor) has a blank piece of paper in front of her, and is trying to sketch a scene that she has never witnessed, which is being described by someone else. She must impose her own ideas as little as possible, simply encouraging the other person to spell out his understanding as clearly as he can. At a later stage, when she has the main features blocked in, she may feel able to ask questions about the details, knowing that even the wrong questions are not going to disturb radically the main outline, which has already been laid down.

There is much more to empathy, because it has emotional elements as well as cognitive ones. The picture has colour as well as shape, if you like. But this brief discussion must suffice for present purposes, because any written account can give only limited pointers to what empathy is like.

## WARMTH

'Acceptance', 'non-possessive warmth', 'unconditional positive regard' – all are phrases used by writers from different perspectives to draw attention to this factor in counselling. At first sight this seems to mean that you have to like your client before you can be any use to him, but it is more complex than this rather impractical emotional ideal.

Rogers (1951) uses the term 'unconditional positive regard': the idea of the 'unconditional' qualification being that the counsellor communicates that there is absolutely nothing the client can do that will put the counsellor off him. It is immediately clear that in the context of supervision, with its elements of authority and accountability, this cannot be true. As we have seen in the contract provisions on confidentiality, it is possible that the staff member could violate ethical or professional principles to the extent that the supervisor would feel obliged to report, discipline, or even suspend him prior to dismissal proceedings.

But none of the above detracts from warmth expressed as *respect* for the other person. Sometimes in supervision this respect comes easily; the supervisor knows that the staff member is doing a good job, or that she is battling against considerable problems and trying to overcome them, and respects her for that. Sometimes it comes less easily; the staff member is obstructive, hostile, ignorant, manipulative, or 'only in it for the money'. She does not seem to respect the supervisor or the clients – so why should one concede to her dignity that she grants to no one else? This is a question only the individual supervisor can answer. One thing is clear; it is a matter less of spontaneous emotion in the moment than of committed general values. If the supervisor's value system includes the notion of respect for others, then he will be searching for that 'hook' in the other person on which to hang his warmth. If, on the other hand, his values see others as primarily means to the achievement of some personal end (for example), then neither his intellectual nor his emotional capacities will be tuned in to this search.

The above may sound relatively easy, but it is not. The ability to sustain warmth rests on two main factors. The first is to do with the supervisor's own state of mind and feeling. If he is frustrated and in the kind of mood where everything has gone wrong and he feels like steamrollering through anything that gets in his way, then respect tends to go out of the window. This affects all of us at some time or another, and it is probably relatively transitory; but it may be only fair to the supervisee to let her know where you are before starting the session (see genuineness, below). The second factor is to do with the capacity to see beyond the immediate behaviour (and values) with which you are confronted. To take the example cited above: the staff member may not be doing the job very well (immediate behaviour), but there are problems in the background, which she is doing her best to work on (what lies behind it). Respect is based in part on the confidence that, when the other problems have been sorted out, she will prove to be a capable, contributing staff member. To understand everything is to forgive anything. We all have different levels of tolerance for this kind of situation, and reach at different stages the point of saying, 'That's no excuse!' That is as it should be; in supervision, outcomes in practice are the important thing, not staff feelings. But a basic orientation towards people that sees them, for example, as problem-solving beings engenders some degree of respect.

A further feature of warmth to look at has been mentioned in passing earlier (pp. 22 and 37; see also Bion 1970): containment. Strictly speaking it is not so much a component of warmth as a consequence of it. It is the quality of a relationship that enables someone to explore healthily his own feelings in the confidence that someone else will make sure he does not damage himself or anyone else in the process. The supervision relationship can provide a container for staff feelings, if it is characterized by warmth. The contract is a structural device to make this containment easier, but it can never by itself bring it about. Containment is available when the staff member feels that 'it's OK to let oneself go in here'. (Sometimes a game is set up in which it is almost obligatory to do so, as in some encounter groups; this does not help.)

The role of the supervisor is to provide the staff member with sufficient protection for him to feel this freedom (see also the notes on the 'regenerative framework' in Chapter 11, 'Learning and Change', page 157). This protection involves not only warmth, acceptance, and security during the session, but also evidence of competence at establishing closure at the end of it. (See the remarks on this in Chapter 6, 'The Supervision Session'.)

GENUINENESS

In many respects, genuineness is towards oneself what warmth is towards the other person. This is neatly expressed in the Transactional Analysis injunction of the 'life-position' that needs to characterize the therapeutic relationship: 'I'm OK, you're OK.' 'I'm OK, you're not OK' may indicate genuineness without warmth; 'I'm not OK, you're OK' shows warmth without genuineness (Harris 1973, Steiner 1975). Only 'I'm OK, you're OK' combined the two.

However, being OK does not mean being perfect. Rather, it implies a degree of comfort with yourself, although not a degree of complacency. It means respecting yourself, in order that you can respect the other person. As usual Jesus got it right when he commanded us to love our neighbours *as ourselves*; if we unpack this statement, it makes it clear that our capacity to love others is directly related to our capacity to love ourselves.

Genuineness is most easily discussed by an examination of its opposite, which is phoniness. Phoniness is the supervisor pretending to be something that she is not – pretending to have more experience of supervision than she has, pretending that she knows where she is going when she does not, or pretending to be her own much-admired supervisor and trying to do it the way he would. It has a number of consequences. First, the supervisor is likely to be caught out. If she has not really got the skill to do something, then she has not got it, and adopting someone else's manner or tone of voice is not going to make any difference. She is likely to get into deep water, in which her mentor might be able to swim, but the supervisor herself is likely to drown. Second, she is likely to be seen through. After all, the staff have a good idea of the kind of person the supervisor is from working with her, and they will certainly notice if she becomes different when they sit down for supervision. And if they see through her, it undermines the security of the whole process and indeed raises questions about the usefulness of supervision. What kind of activity is this if the boss has to play these silly games?

Third, and very practically, the supervisor will be preoccupied. It is difficult enough to be empathetic in supervision anyway, without introducing the intervening stage of asking, 'What would my supervisor (or Caplan, or Kadushin) think of this?' In order to be free to engage with the world of the supervisee, you need to lay your own preoccupations on one side; and in order to do that you need to have a good enough level of comfortableness with yourself. Counsellors are enjoined to stop practising if they have got too much on their own minds to be of any use to anyone else; even in counselling this is a counsel of perfection, and probably even more so in supervision. However, it is something to bear in mind.

Genuineness not only means being psychologically comfortable with yourself. It also has a structural dimension, in that one of the supervisor's attributes as far as the staff member is concerned is his authority. In mentioning administrative supervision, I have made it clear that I do not believe that the structural authority of the supervisor either can or should be set aside within the supervisory session. There are occasions when one would be failing in one's duty if one did not give direct instructions about how something is to be done, or did not convey disapproval of some aspects of practice. If this authority is swept under the carpet, it is likely to emerge as a major problem at some stage, justly provoking the indignation of the staff member that it was not made clear earlier on. Once again, the contract is a great help here. But authority is not just a burden to be borne or a liability within the supervisory relationship. Staff also carry authority in relation to their clients, and the way in which the supervisor handles his authority can be a model as to how they might handle theirs.

## GUIDELINES FOR THE SUPERVISION RELATIONSHIP

Before looking at some of the complications that may arise, it is possible to give some brief guidelines which a supervisor may be able to hold in his head as points of reference to use when checking the state of the supervision relationship.

(1) The first is the primacy of *listening*. Listening is in itself an act of communication; it communicates warmth, it is essential to empathy, and any sign of phoniness interferes with it. So the quality of the supervisor's listening is the best guide to the health of the supervision relationship.

(2) Second, a reference back to Transactional Analysis, and the necessity for an underlying assumption in the relationship that 'I'm OK, you're OK.' Both partners are responsible human beings engaged in an exercise in which their respective roles make no difference to their worth or their competence.

(3) Third, also from Transactional Analysis: the supervision relationship is a set of Adult–Adult transactions. It is not appropriate to go into the details of this here, since there are many excellent books on TA, but the Adult ego-state is the rational part of ourselves. Only in the Adult state can one really listen to another person, and the basic equality of the Adult–Adult relationship is a great help towards the maintenance of the 'I'm OK, you're OK' position. (Transactional Analysis also includes the theory of Games, and these will certainly be encountered in supervision – Kadushin 1976 has a whole section on them. Once you are comfortable with basic supervision, this is an area that well repays further study.)

## LINKING AND TRANSFERENCE

'Linking' and transference both relate to a similar phenomenon, but draw attention to different levels of it. 'Linking', identified and discussed by Caplan (1970), is a process that takes place between the staff member and the client; transference takes place between the staff member and the supervisor; counter-transference takes place between the supervisor and the staff member. In each case, we are dealing with the way in which the present relationship is influenced by the fact that one party (or occasionally both) perceives the other in the same way as she perceived another person in a significant relationship in the past. Usually it involves the unconscious projection of the attributes of the person from the past on to the other in the present. To take some simplified examples:

– A staff member reacts to his supervisor not merely as a father-figure, but as if he were his own father.
– A staff member over-compensates in her relationship with the children for her 'mistakes' in the way she brought up her own children.
– The supervisor's relationship with a female staff member is modified by a barely acknowledged sexual attraction.

## Linking

Linking is the more general case in which either the frame of reference (the way a staff member gives meaning to a situation) or the feelings of the supervisee bear the hallmarks of contamination by an understanding or feeling more appropriate to another relationship or setting. The task of the supervisor is 'unlinking'. Thus, when a member of staff who is being unmercifully manipulated by the youngest child in the group makes an unguarded comment such as: 'Ah, but she's such a wee mite, and when she looks at you with those big eyes . . .' one may suspect that the child has 'tuned in' to something in the staff member that is not entirely appropriate. However, to point this out is not enough; it is necessary to find out what it is. Is it a memory of the staff member's own daughter? Or of a pet puppy? Or a family myth that small size indicated vulnerability? Or what? Only then, by judicious exploration of the staff member's understanding, is there a way to demonstrate gently that here there is something about which to be on one's guard.

Another staff member may have reacted over-harshly to some

routinely undesirable occurrence, leaving clients mystified at his flying off the handle, and fearful of his unpredictability. He may justify it by saying something like: 'If there's one thing I can't stand, it's this stupid teasing.' Why does he feel so strongly about it? Where does that feeling come from? Was he teased as a little boy? Was he the teaser – and did something go terribly wrong with his play? Has he had an unhappy affair with a sexually teasing girl?

There is invariably some kind of recognizable qualitative difference between the linked reaction and that which stems from a genuine conviction about values. On the whole, that difference is to do with the isolated nature of the reaction, which is called forth by one particular set of stimuli but not by other parallel cases. Warmth in this case relates to an understanding of the complexity of the staff member as an individual human being, and an acceptance that such quirks of behaviour are based on the realities of personal history.

## Transference

Transference is more difficult to detect and to work with, primarily because it is more general and less easily acknowledged. It can relate to the internal world of a resident, of the staff member, or of oneself. It can be colluded with, contained, or worked through. It can be felt, on the part of the transferer or transferee, as any emotion one cares to think of. It usually creeps up so slowly that it has acquired an influential history before it is recognized, even by an outsider. When one is inside it, it is weird, mystifying, and utterly compulsive. Take some simple examples:

An otherwise apparently stable girl reacted very strongly to a mature male member of staff when she came back from home leave. She came to him with her troubles, sought physical comfort and reassurance from him, and then would flip into a tantrum and run off making hysterical allegations against him. It later became apparent that there was a history of incest in the family. Here the transference is from the client to the worker, and it clearly has do with the working-through of ambivalent feelings about her father.

An adolescent girl and a female worker happened to share the same name, which tended to draw them together. When the girl became pregnant, however, the worker became obsessed with her, and was determined that she should have the child, against the girl's own inclinations. It was only when the worker had got to the point of offering to adopt the baby herself that it came to light that she had had an abortion at only a little older than her namesake, and had ever thereafter felt it to be a guilty mistake. This may, just about, be linking; but it feels more like a transference, a version of 'I can't let you make the same mistakes I did', rendered many times more powerful for its unconscious element (the worker denied any connections). Technically, the transference was on to the foetus, of feelings about her own dead baby. This is staff-to-client counter-transference.

A young male member of staff from abroad developed a great attachment to his officer-in-charge, an older woman. In mocking formality he would respond to directives with, 'Yes, ma'am!' but said in such a way it came out as 'mum'. When she moved on to another establishment, he was desperate to follow her, and eventually did. A slightly odd but not necessarily destructive transference from staff member to superior here – presumably amplified by the setting of a home for handicapped children.

An older man and a younger man had both done the same qualifying course, and had shared the same tutor. The older man became an officer-in-charge and, a couple of years later, the younger applied for the deputy's job. The older man enthusiastically appointed him, but their relationship deteriorated rapidly from then on. When the younger man could stand it no longer he started to apply for his own establishment, and was undermined on several occasions by lousy references from his officer-in-charge. The older man in this case was the eldest of several brothers, all of whom had overtaken him professionally. There is here a counter-transference from superior to subordinate, amplified by the sibling rivalry of two men who had shared the same college tutor.

Transference is always there in the supervisory relationship, although rarely in as dramatic terms as the examples suggest. Sometimes it helps, sometimes it hinders. It is not always the same; and the study of the changing nature of the transference in such a way as to use the relationship between supervisee and supervisor to illuminate the relationship between the client and the worker has been dubbed the 'reflection process'. The one is the mirror to the other (see Mattinson 1975).

Hints and tips: watch out for irrelevant thoughts and feelings that crop up spontaneously when you are trying to concentrate on the other person; ask yourself, 'What do they say about this relationship, here and now?' The problem is that a thought or feeling does not present itself in one's mind with a label already attached to it saying 'transference'; it puts in an appearance as if it were any other thought or feeling. Nor does the fact that something stems from transference, rather than from 'reality', mean that it can be discounted or set aside. Fantasies can influence action just as much as 'reality' can.

So, what do we do? If transference cannot be discounted, and it can be 'disconnected' only by uprooting it at source, we have a supervision problem. Working on the source material is straying into the province of analytical therapy, and most supervisors do not have the time, the skill, or authority from the supervisee to do this. Equally, there is an implication that transference is in itself a neurotic symptom that requires treatment – which is not so, because it is common to all kinds of relationship, and sometimes fruitfully so. But it cannot just be ignored, so it has to be contained, which in this case must mean drawing attention to its possibility (not always in technical terms) when you think it is around, and trying to set it aside. When it seems to be a component of a staff member's reaction to a resident, for example, check out the evidence from other sources apart from the staff member's feelings. If it seems to be taking place between the staff member and yourself, you can talk about it explicitly as part of 'taking stock' of the supervisory relationship. The aim is not so much to make it go away as to limit its potency, so that practice, both outside and within supervision, is not too drastically affected by it.


PRIVACY

The delicate nature of exploring the transference brings us on to the matter of privacy. Unlike the counselling relationship, in which the assumption is made that a client will derive some benefit from baring all (or at least a fair proportion) of his innermost feelings, supervision is a work-related activity in which the test is the benefit derived by the clients. A staff member is perfectly entitled to object to anything that smacks of 'prying' if she cannot see its direct relevance to the delivery of an effective service to the clients; hence there is a delicate balance to be struck. On the one hand, most of supervision is concerned with performance. As long as this is satisfactory, there is no call to concern oneself with feelings. On the other, supervision does become superficial if it is all conducted on this level, and opportunities for committed learning and change become rather limited. Furthermore, the staff member needs to be at least as genuine with the residents as the supervisor is with her, and if she is unprepared to explore her feelings and attitudes it is unlikely that she will be able to sustain such genuineness.

This is a matter that for once cannot really be helped by the contract, because of how the issue unfolds, and because it is not at all easy to anticipate what it is going to look like until it is actually present. In part, the question of the degree of self-revelation expected in supervision will be determined by the culture of the unit. The rest will be determined by the kind of relationship that the supervision partners establish between them. The rule is therefore that you do not have the authority to explore the inner world of the staff member unless and until she grants it. You do, on the other hand, have authority to demand good work from your staff, and thus to raise questions about any blocks to that kind of performance that may arise.

CONCLUSION

There is a danger that, because I have used the framework of counselling qualities to explore the personal aspects of supervision, I have 'clientized' the supervisee. At times he has come across as a mixed-up, twisted loony. Forgive any exaggeration that may have crept in; it just so happens that simple cases tend to be extreme ones.

There is a simple point to end this chapter on. There are two basic ways of trying to get people to work effectively: pushing and pulling. As with trying to move physical objects, there are times when one is more effective than the other, and neither is right or wrong. Counselling as a model is on the 'pull' side; and in supervision it is worth trying this one first sometimes. For some reason, while we may be prepared both to pull and push residents, I note a general bias in supervision towards pushing all the time. The pull model is put forward as a corrective.

# 11  Learning and Change

While some parts of supervision are concerned with helping people to carry on with what they are already doing, a significant proportion of the time is devoted to getting people to change, in ways great and small. This chapter concerns the management of change in the individual, which is not to say that it has any easy answers. Although people are changing all the time as they grow older and acquire more experience, controlled change is difficult to manage and not fully understood. What follows can be no more than a brief account of adult learning applied to staff supervision in group-care settings.

KNOWLEDGE

Although a great deal of learning theory is particularly concerned with knowledge, it is the easiest kind of learning to manage. In its simplest form there are three things that need to be considered in the structuring of a learning programme: relevance, understanding, and digestibility.

*Relevance*, the first factor, will get only a brief mention here. It is well known psychologically that people learn something more easily if they can see its relevance to something they are already interested in. They may find it difficult to learn nonsense syllables, and soon forget them; but if those syllables take shape for them as phrases in the language of the country they are about to visit for their holidays, it all falls into place and they will learn much more quickly. In fact, if the interest is there, people will learn in spite of the teaching method as well as because of it.

In supervision, it is a reasonable assumption that you can

demonstrate the relevance of everything you want people to learn. It is to do with their job, after all, and it is probable that the staff member himself has raised the issue of his own ignorance, so interest and motivation are not likely to be problems.

*Understanding*, the second element, might require a little more work. People vary in their ability to understand things, and although there are aspects of understanding that have much to do with seeing relevance and being able to digest information, one important feature is the question of whether what I am presented with has an identifiable shape or not, and whether I can find a way into it. Apart from the issue of intelligence, people also vary in the way they learn and understand what they already know; one reason why some teaching methods fail with some people and work with others is to do with the 'shape' in which the material is presented. Some people, for example, are 'serial' learners, who respond best to material presented step by step; others are 'holistic' learners, who like to get the broad shape of an issue and then fill in the details later. Some are 'convergent' thinkers, whose natural tendency is to seek definite and concrete answers to problems; others are 'divergent' thinkers, whose ideas go off in all directions. No style of learning or thinking is 'better' than another for all purposes, and in social work all forms are both needed and found in different members of staff.

So to be effective in helping a staff member to learn, it is important to have an idea of how she learns best. The trouble is that she may well not know, never having given the matter much thought, or having been misled by a label stuck on her in the past of being 'bright' or 'thick'. Such labels may say as much about the fit between her and the teaching approach employed at her school as about her intelligence. After a while you may well find – by trial and error – a learning pattern she will take to better than any other. But to begin with it is best to be prepared to experiment, and not to assume that your own preferred learning style is the only one.

Whatever the shape or pattern the staff member relates to best, it will be found necessary to divide the knowledge up into 'bite-size chunks', so that she does not get indigestion; and also to provide a framework that shows how the chunks fit together and what their contribution is to the whole. The question of pattern is a great deal to do with finding the best kind of framework to present and the best way of chopping up the material into chunks.

*Digestibility*, then, is the third element. It describes the ease with which knowledge may be assimilated, and it has two major aspects. The first is to work out how to pace the learning, and the second how to check that it has been assimilated.

If you are going too fast in the presentation of material, the learner is not going to take it in effectively. Some will be forgotten, and, what is worse, some will get mixed up and confused and create far more problems when you try to sort it out again. Yet you want to go as fast as possible in order to avoid both wasting time and the boredom and loss of impetus that come from the feeling that no progress is being made. This means that there has to be some way of checking whether the knowledge has gone in and stuck or not. As soon as it is effectively remembered and can be recalled at will, go on to the next bit. You can either deliberately bring up case material that gives the staff member the opportunity to parade her newly acquired knowledge, or make a point (and perhaps a note to yourself) to listen for evidence of it in the usual supervision discussions.

## Learning blocks

Unwillingness to assimilate information is a block that occurs at a fairly early stage in the learning process; unwillingness to make use of it comes in later. In either case the blockage can be seen as either cognitive or emotional in origin. Cognitive blocks are those arising when a person already has information in the slot for which the new information is destined. The only problem is that the information already in place is wrong. In the words of Josh Billings, 'The trouble with people is not that they don't know, but that they know so much that ain't so'

(Shaw 1874). True and false information about the same thing do not easily coexist; truth is not necessarily the criterion that determines which bit of information sticks (see the section on theory, above, p. 104). There is 'unlearning' to be done before new learning can take place, and although this is primarily a cognitive process, there can be an emotional component to it as well. There is, however far-fetched as it may seem, an element of loss in giving up cherished old beliefs. Do you remember how you felt when you realized that Father Christmas was just a story after all? Not all beliefs appeal so much to the child or the romantic or other 'deep' parts of ourselves, but we need good reasons to give them up.

Emotional blocks can exist on their own or reinforce cognitive ones. These come into play when one just cannot afford to accept new information, because it calls into question all kinds of other things (see the section on threatening learning, below, p. 155). Some blocks, particularly those that are not obvious, take a long time to remove because they have become so established.

SKILLS

The same kind of analysis may be applied to the acquisition of skills, with the important difference of the centrality of *practice* in skill development. Skill development cannot be hived off to colleges and courses. As a teacher I spend a lot of my time trying to develop role-plays, simulation, and video exercises in an attempt to give people the opportunity to practise skills; but the best that I can do is a very poor substitute for real practice. In the residential setting with real residents there is no simulation, and there is the opportunity for the repetition that is central to practising. Supervision can monitor this learning. But one gets nothing for nothing in this life, and the practice situation has its own problems. First there is the indivisibility of skills in the real world, then the problem of learning the wrong way and having to relearn, and third the associated question of the occasional disadvantage of skill learning, leading to blocks in the same way as in knowledge acquisition. 'Indivisibility' refers to the fact that, while in exercises it is possible to practise one skill at a time and then to try putting them together, in the real world everything has to be done at once.

There is therefore something to be said for courses to get things started, but the build-up and subsequent development have to be done at work. It is a great help to skill development if the supervisor can find ways of containing the uncertain demands of work to enable staff to start as far possible with easy situations and progress to the more difficult. There are several ways of grading the learning of, say, taking a group of clients on an outing. One can go with another member of staff, then take one or two selected residents on one's own, and then perhaps a larger group. When one has developed the skill of having eyes in the back of one's head, holding three conversations at once, and appearing to be relaxed as well, then one can begin to take one or two 'difficult' residents, on their own – and so on. The alternative 'deep end' approach leads only to confidence-shattering disasters on the one hand, and on the other to so many things that can go wrong all at once as to make it impossible to work on them all in supervision.

## VALUES

Values and their associated attitudes are the most difficult aspects of a person to change, and so they ought to be. Values are at the centre of the kind of person one is. My values are reflected in my priorities, and although half the time I may not even know what those values are, they continually translate themselves into practice whenever I make a decision. We have all kinds of words that cover values – ranging from the relatively trivial, which have implications only for ourselves, to the much more important ones, which underpin our whole attitude to the world, our fellows, and our community. We may refer to them as 'tastes', 'opinions', 'beliefs', or 'principles', but to attack or question the more important ones is to attack ourselves.

Values are expressed in constant and commonplace things, which we now refer to (with an unacknowledged debt to Alfred Adler) as 'life-style' – the kind of clothes we prefer, the hair-style we affect, and whether we eat wholemeal bread or not – through to our prejudices and principles such as political or religious opinions. They are reflected in the priorities we attach to our social roles, such as work versus family roles. Given that supervision is not in the business of personality change at a very basic level, working with people's values is the closest we are likely to come to it.

We also have overriding 'meta-values'. If someone declares, like Patrick Henry, 'Give me liberty or give me death!' we find it easy to recognize his commitment, although we may not necessarily share it or understand it. If instead he mutters, 'Well, all right, if you say so', we are not inclined to acknowledge that there is a value commitment there too, even if it is of the order of 'anything for a quiet life'. That meta-value is just as important to an accommodating individual as 'liberty' was to Henry, as lack of bitterness to Edith Cavell, or any of the other well-known examples it is easy to cite. (See the experiments on conformity carried out by Milgram (1973).) Although it is difficult to conceive of anyone going to the stake for the sake of the principle of swimming with the tide, it takes a lot to get such a person to give up that kind of meta-value.

Such values are reflected too in our cognitive understanding of things. Our frames of reference are largely the product of our values, and they are always selective; so some features of what we observe or listen to catch our attention, and others are ignored. If I have a strong political commitment, I may find it very difficult to *hear* what my political opponent is saying. We are back to reasons for adopting particular theories, and cognitive and emotional blocks to learning.

Nor should we ignore the fact that values are also central to the kind of establishment we run (to talk about 'running' an establishment already implies some value-judgement). The energy to run an establishment on any basis other than that of sheer administrative convenience must come from the values held by the staff. (Pause a moment and work out why I say just 'the staff'.) (See Atherton 1984a; Wills 1979.) If values are difficult to confront and change, and they are central to both the individual and the establishment, it should be apparent that the most important thing to look for in recruiting any member of staff is the fit between her or his personal values and those of the establishment itself, because a clash in this particular area is going to be the most difficult to resolve.

Is changing values therefore impossible? Evidently not, because people *do* change them; but we ought to expect it to be difficult and to come into the category of threatening learning, to be discussed below. It is, paradoxically, when the learning is too *easy* that the supervisor has to get worried this time. Moulding plasticine may be much easier than sculpting stone, but it is obvious which is more permanent. If a staff member (other than a new member of staff) appears to change values without protest or defence, then what one is probably encountering is the very effective and resistant meta-value of 'going along with the crowd'. Becker (1970) calls it 'situational adjustment', and contrasts it with 'commitment' or committed change, which is in his view characterized by the existence of 'side-bets' (otherwise known as 'putting your money where your mouth is'). Transactional Analysis notes that situational adjustment occurs when the person who appears to be changing responds from Adapted Child, rather than from Adult or Parent.

There are four main reasons why value change that is too easy is problematic. First, it is likely to result in the staff member saying one thing in supervision and doing another in any unsupervised moments with the residents, the dangers of which are obvious. (However, there are other reasons why this might happen as well.) Second, the staff member is likely to be inconsistent, and inclined to 'back down' from confrontations. This is not always a bad thing, in that flexibility and willingness to admit when one is wrong are characteristics (values) to be encouraged; but it is a bad thing when the reason for backing down is simply that the going gets tough, which is what is likely to happen if the staff member does not *own* the values he is called upon to embody. Third, situational adjustment is fundamentally dishonest; it therefore strikes at the root of what I would hope is a basic value in the establishment: honesty. Fourth, because it is dishonest, it opens the way for the establishment of a destructive subculture, and if this happens then supervision and all other kinds of professional management are threatened.

There is no simple recipe for dealing with problems of values; indeed, it would be dangerous if there were. But respect for the staff member's opinions and attitudes on the part of the supervisor is essential. A dismissive or nagging approach is likely merely to encourage situational adjustment on the one hand, or destructive argument on the other.

So far we have looked at three main *fields* of learning. Now we turn, equally selectively, to *how* people learn.

NON-THREATENING LEARNING

This category covers all the learning that may be hard work, but does not threaten other areas of one's life. It is usually fairly specific to practice, and although the discipline may be unfamiliar, and may even be mildly at odds with the way the learner thinks of herself, fundamentally it is seen as advantageous. Report-writing is a good example. It worries a lot of new entrants to social work, and even some old hands, and it involves both academic aspects and a practical skill (and values will be expressed in the report as well). The initial reaction is often, 'I can't do that. I was never any good at writing essays at school.'

There are three points to bear in mind that will help in setting up and reflecting on a learning programme for this kind of work. The first is to do with *modelling*. In all areas of practice, the most powerful influence of one person, not necessarily the supervisor, on another is that person's practice. It may be admired and emulated, or it may be rejected, but it speaks far louder than words.

The second point to bear in mind is that every task can be

broken down into simpler ones, and that these have to be taken in some kind of order. Develop confidence in one area and then go on to the next; but remember that there is a danger in subdividing everything too simply, which is the possibility of losing sight of the overall shape and objective of what one is up to, so that a component assumes too much importance in its own right. Use the same principles as the formulation of hard contract elements (p. 47) to work up learning objectives for the acquisition of this skill.

Third, people do not improve steadily. Learning curves are not neat upward curves. There are ascents and plateaux, peaks and troughs where people seem to get worse and lose skill instead of acquiring it. This is all a normal part of the learning process. So you should not assume, just because there is a period of rapid development, that you have 'cracked it'. Equally, you should not let yourself, or the staff member, be too discouraged by the fact that she seems to be making no progress at all for a while. In the model that follows learning is presented as a progression through a number of stages, but it should not be thought that that progression is an uneventful one. A graph of progress will be a very wiggly line, with only a general tendency upwards.

THE SOAKING-IN MODEL

One way of looking at learning in social work was put forward some time ago by Bertha Reynolds, and what follows is based on her work (1965). She suggests that learning skills, in particular, is a process of declining self-consciousness about practising them, until they become 'automatic' and second nature. So in the case of driving a car, the learner driver will have to 'think' deliberately every time he changes gear, whilst the experienced driver does it automatically. The important insight of this model is that it emphasizes that being able to do something right once or twice does not of itself mean that you have 'learnt' it; this is not really reached (if ever) until you not only do it right every time, but without having to bother about whether it will be right – being pretty sure that it will come out

OK. At this point, energy is released for attention to other things. For the supervisor, the message is that you do not stop working on something until it is a natural feature of an individual's way of working. It is only then, for example, that a person is likely not to regress or abandon the skill or knowledge (or value position) when subjected to stress. In short, learning is about a changed way of doing things *soaking in*, until it is no longer an unfamiliar accessory tacked on to a person, but part of the very fibre of her being.

### Stage fright

'I can't do it! Help!' This is the point where the new skill is totally unfamiliar and 'alien'. It may last for only a moment, or it may paralyse the learning process for ever. It may be broken by the person being overtaken by events that mean that he has to do *something*; the review creeps inexorably nearer, or the client who has to be confronted is standing in front of him saying sarcastically, 'Geoff says, you want to *see* me.' It may be broken by a word of encouragement: 'Go *on*, then!' The first time is always the worst, and afterwards one realizes that those fantasies about the terrible things that could happen have not been fulfilled, even if one did make one hell of a mess of it. But if there has never been a first time, the stage fright can build up and up into something virtually unconquerable. How does a surgeon go about making her first-ever incision into a living body? I suspect that in many cases she goes into the operating theatre thinking that she is just going to observe one more operation, until the principal surgeon tells the nurse to give *her* the scalpel and says, 'Right, you've watched and stitched up enough. Get on with it.' Whereupon the junior, having no time to think about it, either faints or gets on with it.

### Sink or swim

This is the situation once you are committed. The cut is started, the chairman of the case conference has asked for your views, the client is protesting her innocence or swearing.

You probably forget 90 per cent of what you thought you knew about how to handle this situation, and cling desperately on to some trivial or irrelevant bit of instruction. At some stage you stand back and ask, 'Is it really *me* doing this?' – indicating that it is still pretty alien. But you survive, probably. If you don't, it is going to be difficult to try again; if you do, you can pat yourself on the back first and then kick yourself for all the mistakes, but by then you are on your way.

**Trial and error**

Now that the initial horrors are over, you can begin to experiment and try out different techniques and tactics. Slowly developing confidence in getting through the situation some-how frees energy to give some thought to doing it better. You may even be able to remember some of the advice and instruction, and to test it out. Sometimes the outcomes will be better, sometimes worse. Sometimes the feeling is 'never again!' and sometimes you can hardly wait for the next opportunity. The learner may develop a phoney and brittle confidence, ready to be cast down by the next minor set-back or full-scale disaster. Feelings will swing between highs and lows, blaming others for failure and kicking oneself for incomplete success. This stage may even be accompanied by Walter Mitty fantasies about how good one is going to be; and in some areas of work it is the most dangerous phase, because people do not understand what they are not yet competent to meddle in. Supervision is one of those areas.

**Relative mastery**

By now it is coming right more often than wrong. The occasional disaster is offset against the more numerous successes (except where you cannot afford even a single mistake; the situation is different for the surgeon or the airline pilot, for example). Your average success and confidence are not upset too much. This is the stage most of us reach with most of the skills we acquire and where learning can slow down a great deal, especially if there is a suspicion that to analyse is to destroy.

**Those who can, teach**

Bertha Reynolds (1965) suggests that the fifth and final stage is where one is able to pass on one's skill and knowledge to other people. That seems like an odd finishing-point, because, if ability is worth having, it is worth having in its own right, not simply in order to be able to teach it to others. But from a lateral thinking perspective there is a lot to be said for this idea. Although many teachers are not themselves brilliant practitioners of what they affect to inculcate in others, the ability to teach effectively is certainly one dimension of a fairly complete mastery of one's skill. The important element that this focuses on is the ability to analyse what you are up to without destroying it. It is by now sufficiently a part of you that you can afford to get self-conscious about it again, in order to improve either your own practice or that of someone else. At this stage there is an acceleration of personal learning as well as teaching; it leads to an increased awareness of how inadequate your own practice is, and how, although it may be good enough, it is not perfect. So, far from being an end-point at which the practitioner can rest on her laurels, it is in fact an effective guarantee that she will not.

At each stage in the model, energy is released when a previous stage soaks in and the level of practice becomes automatic. It is up to the supervisor to ensure that the energy is harnessed to continue upwards.

LEVELS OF LEARNING

Learning is not merely a matter of *how* to do things, but also of knowing *when* to do them. As the final stage of the Reynolds model suggests, truly effective learning is not static; it equips you to go on and learn more. In the light of this, supervision is not concerned simply with the acquisition of knowledge or skills, but with encouraging the capacity to learn from experience, or learning how to learn (Bateson 1973).

For many moderately mentally handicapped people, this is the great blockage. They can be drilled to acquire skills, but they cannot learn when to apply them, or how to learn further. Workers with mentally handicapped people know the difficulties, and so frequently have to over-train their clients, to standards that 'normal' people have abandoned. Do you always make the bed in the morning, always put your clothes away, never leave the washing-up? That is because you have the capacity to exercise discretion as to when things do and do not need to be done; without that, rigid rules are necessary. (But see the pioneering work of Feuerstein in this field (1979).)

If I put my hand in the fire, it will get burnt. This is not really learning, but simple, direct experience, or Learning O. If I learn not to put my hand in the fire in case I get burnt, this is Learning I (first order). But if I am in a fire, and decide not to rush out of it, but to stay and get burned in order to save someone else, this is Learning II (second order). Learning I has been subordinated to a higher form of learning. (Not necessarily morally higher, because I may risk getting burned in order to save the proceeds of a bank robbery and ignore a person being burned to death; just logically higher.) If I then reflect on the whole experience, and learn something new about myself in answer to the question, 'What kind of person am I, that I would risk my own life in order to save someone else?' then that subordinates both the other forms of learning, and may be called Learning III – although even Bateson (1973), who suggested this hierarchy, admitted that we do not know very much about Learning III. For present purposes we will stick with Learning I and Learning II.

Learning II, then, is about putting Learning I in context.

Much of supervision is about Learning II, and this is not always easy to manage. To get back to one of the original contract items (p. 49), 'I want to gain more confidence': it was pointed out that this was 'soft', and that for contract purposes it was desirable to unpack it into its 'harder' components. But it was also acknowledged that, even all together, those hard components still do not add up to gaining confidence; the reason is because while 'finding out about establishment policy' and 'surviving crises' are hard, they are also at the Learning I level, while 'gaining confidence' is at the Learning II (or even Learning III) level. This becomes apparent if you reflect on the fact that confidence comes in part not only through having a repertoire of responses to situations to hand, but also through knowing when to apply which kind of response. Any kind of creative work with other people must call for a degree of selection of the options available.

However, I stand by the injunction to make contract items as hard as possible: first, because until you have the repertoire of responses available, and fairly well soaked in, it does not make much sense to choose between them. It is no good trying to decide which piece to play on the piano if you cannot play the instrument in the first place. Second, Learning II is not easy to manage. Sometimes we *acquire* Learning II relatively easily, but we do so in unpredictable situations; so arranging for us to acquire it is a difficult and unreliable process. All the manager of the learning process can do (the term 'teacher' is not the right one here) is set up promising opportunities and encourage the learner to make use of them.

The 'alternative accounts' technique outlined earlier presents such opportunities. More extensively, there are the 'thinking skills' exercises of Edward de Bono (1985), or of course the study of philosophy, which is of its nature concerned with meta-questions, the substance of Learning II. Only the first two of these are in any sense applicable to supervision, but certainly social work education also needs to embrace the third. However, the direct approach is not always the most effective in terms of facilitating Learning II. Modelling, for example, is probably an important influence – if it takes the form of direct imitation, that is only Learning I. But if it goes beyond that, to an appreciation of the principles that underpin the actions of the model, then there is the beginning of Learning II.

THREATENING LEARNING

We come now to the management of change at a more profound level than the simple addition of new knowledge or skills to one's present repertoire. To some readers, the kind of change described here may seem unnecessarily dramatic, but it is included because many supervisors sooner or later encounter staff members who find it difficult to change, often simply because they have been doing things one way for so long that they cannot see themselves doing them differently.

Threatening learning is personal change that has implications for areas of one's life which go beyond the concerns of the present. The model put forward in this chapter is an attempt to bring together various perspectives on such learning, so as to provide an adequate model of the steps that have to be gone through in order for it to come about.

**Supervision and therapy**

The issue of the privacy of the staff member has already been considered in Chapter 10, 'The Supervision Relationship', (p. 139). In considering the possibility of threatening learning, however, it comes up again in a different form.

A care assistant in an old people's home seemed incapable of learning to do simple things acccording to the set procedures. Fortunately for her Head of Home, she was still in her probationary period, but even after six months she seemed unable to pick up basic points – about how to lift people, for example – that every other care assistant had managed to learn in the first few days. It was not that she was unwilling to learn, indeed she was eager for instruction. Nor did she resent being criticized; she always listened intently, and was grateful for having had the point explained again, and resolved most sincerely to do it right next time. Nor did she seem to be lacking in intelligence. But there was some evidence that she found the same problem in the rest of her life; she was continually forgetting her house keys and locking herself out, for example. Although briefly perturbed by each incident, she would make light of it, and laugh at herself for being so stupid.

As well as the question of what could be done about this care assistant (apart from terminating her contract on the expiry of the probationary period, which seemed to be the most likely outcome), what is the right and authority of the supervisor to interfere in what was apparently a coherent, if self-destructive, life-style? In so far as this perpetual game (in TA terms) affected her work, the supervisor had a right to be concerned about it, and to make every effort to change it. In so far as it was 'just her', however, the supervisor had no brief to act as psychotherapist, even if he were competent to do so.

In the model of supervision advocated in this book, the contract provides some kind of safeguard against such probing, but it is not infallible. The experience of social work may have profound and unintended consequences for the character of any of us, but there is a difference between that kind of more or less gentle and gradual erosion of some of our rough corners and the concentrated and deliberate efforts of another person to change us.

Fortunately, the evidence suggests that if such change is to take place (at least, short of 'brain washing' techniques) it can do so only with the co-operation of the supervisee (see Lifton 1961). We know this in any case from the often futile efforts we make to change people in care; in the final analysis, I am relieved that our efforts in that direction are not super-efficient. None the less, we do have to be clear about the right we have to require another person to change in any fundamental way and what is involved in it.

### The 'conversion' model

The following model is compatible with several other approaches to what is involved in getting people to change, but is placed in an unusual format, being based on parallels with religious conversion. It must be emphasized, however, that this is simply because such conversion is one form of personal change, and that the model is about purely secular changes. Although conversion is a form of radical change – of the magnitude implied by the phrase 'being born again' – the same principles can be applied to lesser changes in our ordinary lives. However, it bears repeating that the reason why such change is threatening is because of its implications beyond the specific element(s) of practice that are our major concern.

The model is presented as a series of steps (see *Figure 8*). The essence of it is that it is not possible to proceed effectively from one stage to the next until that stage has been adequately deal with. So this is not a recipe, but an analysis of what happens, which emphasizes the steps that have to be taken *before* the change we usually think of as 'learning' – in other words, unlearning past ways.

*Figure 8* Schematic representation of the 'conversion' model of the natural history of threatening learning

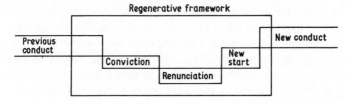

## The regenerative framework

The framework creates *space* for the change to happen. Space, or opportunity, or necessity for change has to be created, and this can happen in any one of three very different ways – the effect being the same (as far as this model is concerned) in each case.

The first and least comfortable or desirable form is found in crises (Caplan 1964; Parad 1965). In a crisis, external circumstances such as bereavement or redundancy create a situation in which it is necessary to readjust one's life-style to be able to cope. In terms of this model, people are plunged into change whether they like it or not, and the regenerative framework is constituted by external events that impinge on them. Although of limited relevance to supervision practice, understanding of crisis theory is useful in all forms of social work.

The second form is that in which, although change is not forced on one by external necessity, it is realized that 'I just cannot go on like this.' In the person's mind, anything is better that the present situation, and so the gates to change are opened by the person herself. A clear example of this is the idea of 'hitting bottom' expressed by Alcoholics Anonymous. As far as AA is concerned, no one can begin the process of recovery from alcoholism until he has understood that he has hit bottom: that any change, however painful, must be better than this. In supervision, this is likely to occur only when dismissal is on the cards, unless the staff member changes; and even then, the threat has to be a psychological reality to the staff member.

The third form is more benign, and the form that will probably be of most importance in supervision. This is the pattern that occurs when the external environment is controlled, so that change can be contemplated and embarked upon without too much risk. If the characteristic of 'hitting bottom' is that you cannot go any further down whatever you do, the characteristic of this kind of permission is the assurance that 'if you fall, I'll catch you'. In some respects it is the diminution of the side-effects of change, and the minimizing of risk.

Thus, if we have a staff member who is a bit of a bully, and we tackle her about it, some of her objections (probably arrived at only after long discussion) may relate to:

(1) colleagues rely on me to keep order; the place will degenerate into chaos if I change my style; and
(2) I'm always like this; I'm just the same at home (and no one ever complains there!).

In this case, provision of the regenerative framework must encourage a demonstration that the fears of (1) are unfounded – which involves the supervision having the strength to make sure that this is so – and also something to deal with (2). It is probably unrealistic to expect the staff member's family to come in on the arrangement, so the task of limiting the risk is to show that change at work does not have to entail a total shake-up of the family structure (however desirable one may see that to be). Providing this kind of assurance is not easy, because we may be tapping into a personality trait that is strongly defended and has served well in the past. However, it is necessary; it is also necessary that the regenerative framework be maintained and perhaps modified to cope with new fears as the process of change goes on.

This third form of regenerative framework, as outlined so far, does not go as far as the two more drastic forms. They embraced their own *activation* for change; in this third form, however, there is no necessary motivation to go ahead and move into it. In this case, there has to be a clear proclamation of the direction of change that is desired, and a corresponding acceptance of it – at some level by the person concerned.

## Conviction

The process of securing acceptance of the desired direction of change is closely tied up with the first step in the internal process of change, which is that the person contemplating it is prepared to 'own' the reality of his present behaviour or attitude. 'Owning' in this case does not simply mean acquiescing to the supervisor's definition of the problem – 'I suppose so, if you say so', muttered without ever meeting the supervisor's eyes. It is a much more positive thing, much more likely to be 'Yes! I *do* do that, don't I!' – a recognition of the reality of present practice without excuses. Since it is often the supervisor who will be putting forward the idea that there is something lacking in the staff member's present practice, it is really more accurate to describe this process as one of *conviction* or *being convinced* of the rightness of the supervisor's view.

This process of getting the staff member to own his present practice is central, and as much time has to be spent on it as necessary. In Chinese 'thought reform' programmes (Lifton 1961; Brown 1963), one of the processes of confession involved getting the deviant to write out his whole life story, and then to have it criticized by the interrogator, and then to write it out again, and again, until he had cast the events in their 'correct' interpretation, and confessed all his offences. That is not advocated here! But it does underline the centrality of this stage, which enables the learner to establish a degree of distance from his previous behaviour.

*Renunciation*

Renunciation involves a recognition of the pay-offs obtained from acting in the 'old' way, which will have to be given up if the new one is adopted, and the preparedness to renounce them. This is the stage most often, disastrously, neglected. It is neglected because under the first two conditions of the regenerative framework it is hardly noticeable.

What are pay-offs? I hesitate to use the term 'rewards', because many of them are pretty bizarre if seen as rewards. Perhaps the more neutral behaviourist term 'reinforcement' fills the bill, but even that implies something enjoyable. Pay-offs are the psychological consequences of ways of behaving, and we have TA to thank for showing more clearly than any other framework that they are not always 'nice', but it may still be hard to give them up. TA talks about people having 'favourite feelings', which are not necessarily pleasant, but the kind of feeling that we have had so often that we are comfortable with it, and when in doubt or under stress we tend to go back to it. It may be anger, or fear, or depression, or any of a host of more sophisticated feelings. Perhaps we are more comfortable feeling 'hard done by' than feeling we got our just desserts; if so, then we will find it difficult to give up behaviour that leads to this kind of pay-off.

In order to make the transition from this stage to the next, the staff member has to be assured not only that she can survive without her present pay-offs, but also that the alternative is really better than the present. The staff member is in the position of a person who is hanging on to a ledge on a cliff with the tips of her fingers. Someone dangles a rope beside her, and tells her to let go with one hand and grab the rope. She may or may not be able to do this; it depends on her confidence in the person holding the rope, and on how long she can hang on to her existing ledge. What assurance does she have that, in attempting to transfer to the rope, she will not just plummet to her death on the rocks below? This is where the regenerative framework and the potency of the supervisor are again important, because although the supervisor is encouraging committed change, he must also provide as much assurance as practicable that the ultimate pay-offs will be greater than the present ones.

At this point it is likely that more pay-offs for the 'old' pattern will become evident. Our staff member had thought that the principal difficulty in giving up her bullying manner was to do with force of habit and lack of confidence in other staff; but now she realizes that she has a great fear of gentleness and closer involvement with other people, because it entails being vulnerable. The supervisor now has a difficult decision to make (in conjunction with the staff member). Do we give up and go back, in the belief that what we may open up is more than we shall be able to contain? Or do we go on? If one gets this kind of situation (which is very rare), it is perfectly honourable to give up. A person taking on supervision does not automatically become a psychotherapist. But it is important to see what one is getting into *early enough*; it is not fair to open something up and then not be able to close it again.

In this stage of renunciation and the beginning of the next stage, the supervisor should be prepared to see the staff member's practice deteriorate, and to support her through this and other possible 'symptoms'. She is disoriented and confused without her old way of working to fall back on, and she needs her supervisor's warmth to convince her or remind her that it is worth it.

## New start

All the foregoing is concerned with freeing the staff member from her past; 'unfreezing', as Lewin called it (1947). It is only now that one can move in to the well-charted waters of learning new responses and ways of working. Most texts on adult learning lay greatest emphasis on this stage, and we can find a wide variety of techniques, from behaviour modification through simple and step-by-step practice, to ordinary advice and encouragement, which will help in making the first steps in a different style of working.

Someone at this stage is vulnerable. Failure now can easily knock them down the stairs again to where they were before, and climbing them a second time is much more difficult than the first. So reaching this final stage does not mean that as supervisor you can give up, and regard the job as effectively done. In the first place, the learning of the new skill or strategy requires careful planning according to basic educational principles; and second, the regenerative framework needs to be maintained until such time as the staff member can survive without it. Success at this stage is imperative. However clumsily the new line of action is pursued, it must be rewarded – preferably by the direct pay-off of seeing it work, but, if that is not possible, by recognition and approval from the supervisor. If all of this sounds intense, and even childish, remember that in working in this new way the staff member *is* a child. He will grow up very fast, and in a matter of days or weeks may gain all the confidence in the new way that he had in the old; but even so, first steps are faltering. However, for this stage refer back to the sections on non-threatening learning. The trauma was in the conviction and renunciation stages, and it should all be plain sailing from now on.

CHOOSING CHANGES

If we go back to crisis theory for a moment, one of its intentions is that the successful management of one crisis enables the person to face the next one with enhanced capabilities and confidence. Certainly this seems to be true in common-sense experience; we wonder admiringly at those people who have been beset with terrible problems in their lives and have come through them all in such a way that they can take in their stride anything that life seems to throw at them. On the other hand, others are completely knocked flat by the first minor hiccup in an otherwise smooth existence. The lesson of this for supervisors engaged in encouraging staff to manage difficult changes is that the successful experience of changing on one occasion provides a good basis for subsequent change. People might even get a taste for it. Therefore, start with something simple and not too threatening. It may be that some aspect of a staff member's personal style and character shouts out as the most important thing to change, but restraint is indicated. Start with something simple where there is a great chance of success.

'Simple' in this case refers not merely to a lack of complexity in the issue being worked out, but also to its minimal involvement with other areas of the staff member's life. In other words, the chances of success are highest if the behaviour focused on is confined primarily to work, and does not extend into home or leisure life. The question of a supervisor's authority to call for change in a whole life-style has been mentioned before, and that is still relevant, but another factor comes in here. If the change in question is confined to work, it may still be difficult for the staff member, but there is a better chance of managing the regenerative framework by creating the space for the change to happen. Outside work, at home or with friends, there is probably little chance to do that.

Thus, if a staff member has two major 'faults', one of which is a generally patronizing and sexist attitude towards women, and another of which is a tendency to wriggle out of writing anything, the second feature is the one to work on first. He may need the experience of success in tackling a less threatening issue before he can even contemplate the possibility of working on something that is a major feature of his values and life-style.

Threatening change that extends into another area of a person's life is fortunately rarely called for in supervision. But changing of lifelong working habits is called for, as the social work environment and its demands continue to change.

Sometimes it has to be undertaken self-consciously according to a programme such as that set out here; sometimes it just happens. In any case, I would suggest that the model will also be found to account for the processes that have occurred informally to make it possible. It should go without saying that the model applies equally to work with clients (once one has sorted out the ethical issues).

# 12 Supervising Students

Supervising a student is similar to supervising a permanent member of staff, with two variations:

(1) There is a third party to the contract: the college.
(2) Placements are for a predetermined period.

This chapter is therefore mainly about the implications of these factors, which have to be considered in addition to everything that has gone before.

## The place of the placement

For present purposes, most of these remarks concern practice placements from Certificate of Qualification in Social Work courses. Other types of course have slightly different requirements, and these need to be checked with the course concerned. But whatever the variations, the same principles apply in managing the placement.

Present CCETSW regulations governing CQSW courses insist that half the time is spent in practical placements. This means both that placements and their matching to individual students are very important, and also that a considerable burden of teaching is placed on the fieldwork teacher or placement supervisor. The objectives that each course specifies will vary – between courses and between placements at different stages of the programme – but it is up to the college to make its requirements clear, and up to the placement and the supervisor in particular to decide whether or not they can be met.

Broadly speaking, placements come in two 'intensities' and two patterns, and each of these places slightly different demands on the student and the host establishment. The intensities are:

(1) *The observation and appreciation placement.* It is common practice on a number of courses to place students in a social work setting with which they have not hitherto been familiar, towards the beginning of the course. This gives them both an experiential base from which to appreciate what colleagues from different settings are talking about, and a chance to test out their own skills in a different context. Further, it raises questions about the extent to which social work is really a generic discipline. Such placements are generally shorter than the more intense ones, and the college objectives will lay greater stress on learning by observation than on participation. Although it makes sense to start supervising students by taking them on observation placements first, this is not necessarily an easy option. The only direct experience many fieldworkers have of work in a residential or day-care setting may have come from their placements many years ago, and so one may be forming impressions that will have a lasting impact for many years to come.

(2) *The career placement.* There may be one or two career placements, perhaps starting towards the end of the first year of a two-year course and continuing to the end of the course. The choice of career placement is often made on the basis of the setting in which the student intends to work after qualification (which may well be the same as the one she came from). The placement may total the equivalent of six months' full-time work, and can easily be a quarter of the student's total training experience, so it is a heavy commitment. Consequently, the matching of the student and the placement needs to be done very carefully.

Either of these forms of placement may be organized in *block* or *concurrent* patterns.

– As the name implies, a *block* placement is full-time. The structure has the advantage for a residential or day-care establishment that a student can be rota-ed in the normal way, and will be witness, as much as any other member of staff, to the daily change and development in the life of the group. However, the other pattern has been favoured for field-based placements, because it permits following through a restricted case-load over a longer period; and since group-care and fieldwork placements have to occupy the same slots in the timetable of most courses, the block placement is relatively rare on generic courses.

- The *concurrent* placement, as its name implies, takes place concurrently with attendance at college. The time spent in the establishment may vary from one day a week to four days a week (there may be block periods included as well). One implication of this pattern is that placements have to be found within reasonable travelling distance of the college, which can severely restrict the choice available to the tutors. Another is that monitoring the placement from the college end is easier, since it is not totally reliant on visits by tutors. However, the potential supervisor should be aware that she will be obliged to find times for supervision sessions that fit in with when the student is on the premises, and this can be an additional constraint.

Even this simple outline of the structures shows that having a student can place considerable demands on the establishment. So the first question to be answered is, Should we take a student at all?

## THE DECISION TO TAKE A STUDENT OR NOT

It can be flattering to be asked to take a student. Some establishments even regard it as a sort of 'seal of approval' on their work from the college. (From the experience of negotiating and visiting some eight hundred placements in my time, I can assure you that it ain't necessarily so!) So there is a great temptation to say 'yes', even when it is not really convenient.

Taking students is merely a sideline to the major task of the establishment, which is to care for clients, and the impact of introducing a student into the prevailing social system needs to be thought through carefully. The presence of a new face is often very welcome, and both student and clients benefit from the experience; but there are occasions when students are inappropriate. If the establishment has just been through a series of crises and is only just settling down; if there is a high staff turnover; if the staff team is not cohesive enough to be able to work with a temporary colleague in such a way that she can learn positive things; if adequate supervision cannot be guaranteed – all these are sufficient reasons for deciding not to take a student. The college, and the agency training section, may put pressure on, but ultimately it is in no one's interests to take students when the setting is not able to receive them adequately.

If the establishment is used regularly by a particular course, it is also wise to regard it as an obligation to ensure that the course is accurately informed about the present state of the unit. The college may use any particular placement only once a year; many things can change in that time, but it may not know about them. If someone else will be supervising, if there has been reorganization, if the needs of the clients are slightly different from this time last year, it is good practice to let the college know so that it will be matching a student to the establishment as it *is* – not to a fantasy of what it was like a year ago.

## THE THREE-WAY CONTRACT

There are now three parties to the supervision contract: the establishment (represented by the supervisor), the college (represented by the student's tutor), and the student herself. This increased complexity makes the contract itself more important than ever.

Usually, the first round of negotiations starts with the college course sending the establishment a set of papers outlining its view and expectations of a student placement.

This may be difficult to read and digest, because it may also serve other purposes; it may be intended for students themselves, it may be part of the material sent to CCETSW for review purposes, and it may even be the kind of quasi-legal document that sets out the criteria for assessment. It may ask for the moon. It is then up to the placement to reply, setting out in response what it can offer. If this can be negotiated satisfactorily, the placement is on – in principle.

Next, the individual student comes on to the scene (perhaps a month or a fortnight before the placement is due to begin). The establishment will receive information about her, often giving basic biographical details, an account of previous experience, and a short report of special interests, needs, or personal learning objectives for the placement. This too is effectively part of the contract. The placement may wish to object to the particular student, or to seek reassurance on particular issues. It is better if all this is done in writing, but things are often messier than that, so nasty surprises can be avoided if undertakings are entered into *only* by the supervisor, and if staff in the office have instructions not to commit themselves to anything without consulting. In short, the same rules apply as to any other transactions across the boundary of the establishment.

Next, there should be a pre-placement visit, attended at least for part of the time by the tutor, especially if the supervisor does not know her. This gives an opportunity to dispel fantasies about the establishment, and about the student. Her anxieties will be greatly allayed if she can be given a copy of her rota for the next few weeks, and the dates and times of supervision sessions. She and the tutor also need to know about any special events that are coming up during the course of the placement, and what role if any she will be expected to take in relation to them. A group of residents is going on holiday; will she be expected to go or not? If she goes, who pays the extra expenses? There will be an open day on one of the days when she would normally attend college; can she be free to attend? What is the college view about working weekends and taking time off in lieu? Then there are the more routine aspects, which are still very important for a student as they are for a client; is there accommodation on the premises? If not, where will she stay? What are the insurance arrangements? Will she be cleared to drive the minibus? Can her vegetarian diet be coped with? What about sleeping-in requirements? What facilities are there for study, and is time specifically made available for it? And the key question: What is the role of a student?

## THE STUDENT ROLE

On placement in a fieldwork setting, the student is usually given a small, controlled, and carefully supervised case-load, together perhaps with the opportunity to participate at an agreed level in such activities as group work. The group-care setting is rather different, in that the practitioner's involvement is not with a discrete set of cases that can be increased or cut almost at will. In a group-care establishment the practitioner becomes a member of a group, with an impact on everyone at once, and the question arises how her formal role can be constituted so that she can learn and contribute, but not be drawn in to the extent that she loses her objectivity. The various 'standard' roles do not quite fit; she is not a client, not a domestic, and not a full member of staff. Some establishments insist that a student is to all intents and purposes a full member of staff, but then run into trouble if something goes wrong and the question is asked, 'You mean to say you let this group of residents go on this trip with *only a student* to supervise them?' The Head of Home can plead in vain that this student had five years' experience and knew more about working with mentally handicapped people than any of her permanent staff – the action is still seen as irresponsible. The 'full member of staff' strategy is also unfair on the student, who needs to be able to stand back and scrutinize her own practice and that of the establishment, in order to learn more than she would if she were working routinely.

At the other end of the scale is the 'only an observer' strategy. That too is unrealistic, because it effectively forbids students from making any contribution at all (in a way that residents may in any case not understand), and denies them the opportunity to test out their skills. What is required is a formula that is manageable and comprehensible to student, staff, and residents, simple enough to be held in the head and referred to when necessary by the student, but flexible enough to cope with unexpected eventualities.

The exact nature of that formula will vary from establishment to establishment, and from course to course. Some placements from Certificate in Social Service courses, for example, are project-based. It is negotiated between all the parties (including in this case the agency management) that the student is there to initiate and develop a particular piece of work, and has full responsibilities in that area, but minimal ones in others. Beedell (1970) describes just such a piece of work he did when on sabbatical from his university. It may be a form of groupwork, or a special programme for a few clients, or the development of an establishment-wide activity. It may even culminate in a definite event, like two or three residents moving to independence, or even a play or a summer fair.

In other situations it may be desirable to set out the boundaries in other ways – perhaps in terms of time. 'You have a free hand to initiate any activities, and carry through any discipline consistent with unit policy, *as long as it is complete and all ends are tied up by the end of the shift.* Anything that goes beyond that must be checked out with a senior member of staff first.' Or: 'You can take up the role of a member of staff as far as anything within the four walls of the establishment is concerned, but anything that goes across the boundaries (relations with the wider agency, or with relatives, for example) must be checked with senior staff.'

### Arrival

Having negotiated all the above, the student will arrive. The point of all the previous clarification is not merely to have all the loose ends tied up in a bureaucratic fashion, but also in part to enable the student to manage the transition on to placement as efficiently as possible, and to be free to get on with the important business as soon as possible. In new and uncertain situations, many students – however competent in their own work-places – regress and lose temporarily some of their working skills. The greater the uncertainty, the more likely this is to happen and the longer it takes to overcome it. Simple issues (such as where one finds a cloth to mop up some spilt tea) loom large, and although there is a limit to the speed at which information can be digested, this needs attention. The supervisor (or perhaps a member of staff with whom the student has been paired for the first few days) needs to see him frequently (as often as once per shift) for brief induction and orientation sessions.

The alternative approach is the 'deep-end' one, which is reported with pride by some supervisors. It has been known (in the old days) to consist of a brief 'hello' followed by the housemother of a family group going off on holiday for a week with her own family, and the assistant housemother not due back until after the weekend. It may make or break a student, but that is not what placements are all about. In short, it has nothing to recommend it.

**The student's placement career**

This section is an application to the placement of Chapter 6, 'The Supervision Session', and in particular of the section on the career of supervision (p. 68). A similar pattern may be seen in many placements as a whole, not just the supervision sessions.

(1) The first stage, which may overlap with the second, and can last from a few minutes to more than a week, is the stage of *disorientation* described above. The student is likely to regress, and it is not to be expected that one will get a true picture of his capabilities. The regression may be expressed in whatever form of defence the student characteristically uses: retreat from engagement with clients, throwing weight about, seeking reassurance, and so on.

(2) The *honeymoon* lasts as long as the residents find a novelty value in the student, and the student finds it in the establishment. Supervision needs to concentrate on the way the student and everyone else may exploit his ignorance.

(3) *Testing-out* is the most easily recognized phase of the placement. Both clients and colleagues will try to get the measure of the student; if control is a significant issue with the client group, this will probably be at the centre of the testing. How the student fares at this time sets the tone for the rest of the placement. If he rapidly shows that he is an 'old hand' and 'up to all the tricks', it will be over and done with, and he can concentrate on other things. If he proves to be naïve or manipulable, it can last for the duration of the placement, and supervision will be dominated by it. A seeming member of staff who presents no boundaries and is unpredictable in working style leaves both clients and colleagues feeling insecure, and undermines not only his own work but sometimes that of the rest of the staff team as well.

(4) The *routine* phase is likely to be the longest, and incorporates the doldrums and the natural phases of staff supervision. It is the period for the consolidation of learning, for checking whether that first flush of energy and enthusiasm can be maintained, and also for the specialized parts of the placement, such as the projects, the visits to court, the meetings with fieldworkers and other visitors.

(5) Experience suggests, however, that just as the doorknob syndrome applies in the individual session, so it also occurs in the placement. Almost regardless of the length of the placement, new things begin to happen in the final fortnight. It may be that the imminence of the ending pressures student and supervisor to get some things done that have hitherto been neglected; it may be that the security of the end in sight enables the student to take some risks. There are all kinds of reasons for it, but frequently there is a need to step up the intensity of

the supervision sessions, to exploit the situation.
(6) *Departure* may overlap with stage (5), in that it has an impact as soon as it becomes a psychological reality to clients and permanent staff. There are all kinds of ways of managing it, from leaving without saying 'goodbye' to anyone, to fantasy assurances for future visits. For some students, the fact that they have to leave serves as an excuse throughout the placement for never getting involved; others deny it completely and start things they can never finish. There needs to be a process of constructive disengagement, and it is up the supervisor to monitor this for the sake of the community as well as the student.
(7) *Follow-through* helps the continuation of learning, as the placement is reflected upon and the experience is used back in college. The burden of this routinely falls upon the tutor, but if the supervisor can be involved too, so much the better. A post-placement visit, or a chat at a supervisors' meeting in college, can be a worth-while investment.

### The tutor's visit and supervisors' meetings

Placement periods are hectic for tutors. They have to combine travelling fairly regularly to a dozen or so establishments and area offices with a teaching load with the students left in college. So fixing mutually convenient times to visit is often difficult, and this creates the possibility for all kinds of games between the triad of student, tutor, and supervisor. The important thing about the supervisor's role is to be prepared for the visit, which includes not only making time to see the tutor and for a three-way session, but also finding a framework within which to explain to the tutor how she sees the student's work and progress. A great deal will have happened to the student and between student and supervisor that the tutor will not know about, and with the best will and skill in the world it is difficult to walk into a group-care establishment and to get the measure of what is going on in a few minutes or hours. The tutor needs some 'hooks' on which to hang his discussions with the student, and all but the most sensitive students tend to externalize problems into failings of the placement itself. The experienced tutor will be aware of this kind of defence, but often has little idea what it is a defence against; the supervisor probably knows the answer to that.

Whether the supervisor sees the tutor on his own or not will depend on preferences and normal practices. There are arguments on both sides.

The other important element in continuing contact with the college is the supervisors' meeting. Constraints of time and other commitments (and whether the supervisor can claim travelling expenses) often mean that the attendance at these meetings is poor, which is a pity. Such events not only permit supervisors to see tutors on their home ground, and perhaps to build up a clearer picture of the course itself, but also enable them to discover areas of common concern. Occasionally colleges make demands on placements and supervisors that are unrealistic, but they never find out because the supervisors all think that they have individual problems with the requirements. The supervisors' meeting, properly conducted, provides an opportunity to engage in a dialogue with the college, between the partners in the programme, that can result in significant changes in policy and practice. It also gives one a chance to pick up ideas from others and generally to raise one's game in supervision. If the college runs a preparation course for supervisors, so much the better.


ASSESSMENT AND REPORTS

One of the major topics of discussion at such meetings is often the matter of assessment and reports. College practices vary, but they have in common the need for a comprehensive and constructive report on the student's performance, which has two purposes:

(1) To contribute to the final assessment.
(2) To identify learning objectives for the future.

The second is important, even when the course ends with a placement, as many do. Students should not stop learning when they leave a course; in fact they should just be beginning. Everyone can contribute some ideas to the direction of that learning.

Some requirements for reports set out specific questions to be answered. This has the virtue of ensuring some fit between the college's concerns about the student and the report itself. But it should be borne in mind that the questions are generalized, and that specific comments on issues that are not asked about should be added at the end. Other colleges leave the form of the report open, in which case the following guidelines may be of help.

(1) Identifying information, including name of supervisor as well as that of student, etc.
(2) Brief sketch of establishment, for those (such as external assessors) who may never have heard of it.
(3) Form of placement, including any special features negotiated at the beginning, references to student's personal learning objectives, and the student role within the establishment.
(4) Brief historical account of the placement, including notes of when supervision took place, any significant incidents, planned or unplanned, and so on.
(5) Relationship of happenings and performance to college's specified learning objectives, and students' own.
(6) Student's relationships and performance with clients.
(7) Ditto with colleagues.
(8) Use of supervision.
(9) Overall comments.

Several issues arise about the preparation of reports, which deserve comment:

(1) Make sure that you write a report, and that it is sent in as soon as possible after the end of a placement. Apart from the problems that it causes to the course not to have a report to hand, delay leads to selective forgetting on the

part of the supervisor, and also makes the student feel as if she is not valued.

(2) Be honest. Some supervisors fudge issues in reports because they discuss them with the student and they do not want to part on a strained note. Some wait until the student has gone and then say all the nasty things they could not say to her face. Some try to be nice because they are afraid that the student will fail if they tell the whole truth, and they do not want that responsibility. Assessment is based on the cumulative evidence of tutor's reports, assignments, supervisors' reports from a number of placements, and perhaps examination results. If a failing grade is possible, most courses go out of their way to make sure that they have a very experienced supervisor for the final placement. The interests of the student and the service as a whole (and future clients) are best served by the supervisor ploughing as straight a furrow as possible, and just allowing his remarks to stand alongside all the other evidence, to be interpreted as a pass or fail by the examiners' meeting, which has *all* the evidence in front of it.

(3) Assertions and comments should always be supported by evidence. Placement reports are discussed in tutorial, and sweeping generalizations can easily be written off by students as saying more about the supervisor than about the student. So whether the effect is positive or negative, reports of incidents and contexts are always needed.

(4) One of the most effective ways of ending the placement is to write the report jointly with the student, or to allow her to discuss it within supervision. However, remember that the report is essentially the supervisor's work, and the responsibility must not be ducked. If the college wants a personal account from the student, it will ask for one.

(5) The report is about this particular student, at this stage in training, in this particular establishment with this staff team at this stage in its life with this group of clients. Assessment is about this student, who will be working in

an as yet unknown post in an unknown establishment (or area office), with unknown colleagues and unknown clients. The task of translating evidence from one into learning for the other lies with the tutor and the student herself.

# 13 Group Supervision

Group supervision has already been mentioned as a possible supervision strategy, with a brief comparison of what it is good at and not so good at. This chapter will expand on the discussion and examine how supervision can be practised in groups.

There are two basic reasons for choosing to undertake group supervision, and they lead to different approaches in practice, so they need to be explored in a little detail. The distinction is between supervision *in* groups and supervision *of* groups.

## Supervision in groups

The usual reason for choosing to supervise in a group is simply that it is the only way to make sure that everyone gets the supervision they need. Take an old people's home, which has the traditional staffing structure of four 'officers' and a large number of hourly paid and probably part-time care assistants. There is no way in which the senior staff can find the time to see each care assistant for an individual supervision session with sufficient frequency to make supervision in any sense meaningful. The obvious solution is to see a number of them together; but the objectives of supervision remain much the same as if it were on an individual basis. There is a sense, therefore, in which supervision in groups is a second-best option. But if it loses certain of the advantages of the individual session there is at least the potential for gaining others. Each member may gain some 'spin-off' benefit from the work being done with others; one person's perceptions may be checked out with the others present so that fantasies can be countered; and there is greater scope for the use of exercises.

## Supervision of groups

The decision to supervise as a group usually comes from a different train of thought. The nature of the caring task in the old people's home referred to above is *discrete*; that is, the staff work in parallel, alongside each other, doing very much the same kind of things, rather than complementing each other. For many of the things that care assistants do (although not for many other things), the residents may see them as interchangeable. Mrs Evans may prefer to be bathed by Mrs Foster, but only because she is gentle about it – technically, anyone else could stand in for Mrs Foster. In other settings, however, staff roles are much more closely linked with each other. Working styles, relationships, and individual skills are so interwoven that it makes more sense to see the *team* as the caring agent, rather than any one individual, just as the behaviour of an ant colony as a whole is more meaningful than that of each ant (see Hofstadter 1983). In work with some children and some mentally disordered people, this even goes to the extent of each staff member being little more than a stereotyped cardboard figure; only the team (or perhaps the residential community as a whole) is real. In such circumstances, it is the team that needs to be supervised, preferably with the back-up of individual supervision as well.

Such a distinction makes it clear that group supervision practice can operate at least at two levels, and probably at many more in between, and the style of supervision will be different in each case. In the former, we basically have individual supervision in public, with the dynamics of the group subordinated to that task. In the latter, what is happening – both inside and outside the session – between the group members is a central topic.

There are, however, certain common features, and we shall look at these first:

(1) Group supervision, like individual supervision, is an uncommon experience. When confronted with uncommon experiences we have a tendency to try to remake them in the mould of something familiar. We may be familiar with the group setting in staff meetings, training courses, or even encounter groups, and know how to behave in those sessions. The supervisor and the members together therefore have the task of making sure that supervision is distinct from any of these. There are many ways in which this can be done, and the more that can be used, the better. The composition of the group can be different from any other in the life of the establishment; the physical setting can be different (different room, different layout of furniture); there can be reminders in physical form – such as the group contract on the wall, or even a conch (see Golding's *The Lord of the Flies* (1954)) if appropriate. There may be rituals and procedures that are distinctive, and the style of leadership must be different.

(2) A degree of mutual trust is essential. While supervisor and supervisee need to trust each other in the individual session, it is easier to trust one person than many. Confidentiality may be maintained within the boundary of the group, but members still have to risk exposing themselves to each other as well as to the supervisor. The less formal a group is, the more trust members have in each other – just consider how much they will open up to each other over coffee in breaks – but the issue arises very rapidly in any formally constituted session, and can dominate the proceedings for ever.

The problem is amplified if the group, as in supervision, is not completely voluntary. Even when staff trust each other implicitly in working together, something happens when they sit down to discuss that work. There is no easy answer. Even the contract only scratches the surface, and trust cannot be legislated for with the best will in the world. It has to be allowed to grow, and this means a succession of good experiences within the level of risk that members are willing to take at that time. Confidence in the ability of the supervisor to contain threatening situations, and not to push too hard too soon, is an important component; without it someone else will take on the role of brake-man, and may never relinquish it. (A useful topic when this comes up is to look at the extent to which staff ask residents to trust them, and whether there are any reasons why they should, apart from there being no alternative.)

(3) Some people talk more than others. This is not just a feature of any particular group but a mathematical rule (Robinson 1984). There are all kinds of reasons for it, but the voluble member and the silent member will not be eliminated. At one level it does not matter, and you can get terrible hang-ups if you worry too much about it. Everyone is responsible for his own actions (and inaction) even in the group setting; and although it is the leader's responsibility to create the conditions within which everyone can contribute (which may include sitting on some members occasionally), she is not responsible for their unwillingness to do so. What is important, however, is that silent members in groups do not use other channels outside the group to make their views known, and thereby undermine the supervision. You are free to challenge that. The silent-member role is probably the clearest aspect of the hidden agenda of the group, which everyone will notice, but it is not necessarily the most influential part.

## SUPERVISION IN GROUPS

### The constitution of the group

For this kind of group supervision, the group concerned does not necessarily correspond with any natural grouping within the establishment, although there may be occasions when, say, two care assistants work together frequently in an old people's home and are supervised together. The supervisor is not therefore tied to any particular size of group, and the general rule can therefore be: make it as small as possible. How small this is will depend on the establishment, the size of the overall staff group, the number of senior staff available to supervise, and the frequency of supervision desired. In any case, it is necessary to set a limit of about four or five supervisees. Any more than this, and you lose the necessary intimacy and personal involvement with the task. The broad mathematical rule is that the amount of responsibility felt by any member for the success of the group will be the reciprocal of the number of people in it. If there are four people, my share is one-quarter or 25 per cent. That is about the minimum that can be sustained for supervision to work; it is a matter of not merely the sense of 'ownership' of the programme that is desirable, but also of the likelihood of it having any influence outside the group sessions themselves.

There are swings and roundabouts in the argument over the desirability of having a group of people at a similar stage in their professional development versus having those who are different. It is clearly necessary to have supervisees who are doing similar jobs, because the concerns of the cook are not likely to be the same as those of the care staff. But if some care staff are more sophisticated in their approach than others, everyone may benefit from the help they can give to those who are either relatively new or not very thoughtful about their work. The act of taking a co-supervisor role can help to develop the thinking of staff as much as others may be helped by them in that role.

On the other hand, there are likely to be issues of concern to the 'more advanced' staff that may lose or bore the others, and so the supervisor in her capacity as chair of the meeting has a difficult balance to strike. If all the supervisees are at the same level it may be easier to establish the group contract and keep things in step, but the burden of supervision falls much more on the designated supervisor and there is a tendency for the sessions to become more management-oriented – even nagging sessions – with less experienced members. The whole thing would be much easier if one could be sure that those who do not know much would keep quiet and be led by those who do!

However, experience shows that assertiveness and dogmatism in groups have little to do with expertise, and it may well be that balancing the personal characteristics of the group members is more important than such variables as their experience or training.

## Method

The traditional distinction in working with groups is between the *task* and *maintenance* levels at which the group operates. The task concerns what the group is set up to do: in this case, supervision; the maintenance level concerns the creation of the climate among the group members that allows it to happen. Supervisors are concerned with both aspects of the work even in the individual session, but in groups the maintenance side assumes greater importance, and can either contribute greatly to task performance or bring it to a full stop. Although there are many different ways of understanding and handling the maintenance side of things, for present purposes we can concentrate on two different strategies.

The first is what is normally encountered in large and formal meetings: the use of rules of procedure to ensure that everyone has an equal say, that decisions are democratically arrived at, and that business is dealt with as efficiently as possible. The formal rules of debate are totally inappropriate to supervision, but there is something to be gained from the adoption of any structure that is comfortable and unobtrusive enough, while still effective enough, to enable the kind of exchange of views, support, and learning that is the essence of supervision.

The second strategy is to interpret what is going on between the members and bring it to the surface so that it can be looked at. This is generally adopted in therapeutic and training groups, and calls for a degree of skill on the part of the group conductor, particularly if he has to combine this with supervision as generally understood. If it can be carried off, the combination is potent – not only in the sense of being powerful, but also sometimes in the sense of leaving people reeling when they come out of the session. There is a third major strategy, or default position, which is to ignore the issue altogether and to struggle on despite any interference from maintenance problems until a crisis arises and something has to be done about them, but the assumption is that this is probably not desirable.

The most effective method, then, calls for a suitable combination of the interpretation and the structure strategies. Each group supervisor will doubtless find one that is to her liking, but the following model is put forward as a starting-point. It is based on some of the more structured approaches to group therapy and therapeutic community models (see Berne 1966b; Douglas 1976; Whiteley and Gordon 1979).

(1) Not only do individuals have contracts, which are negotiated in the group, so that other members can make contributions to them, but the group as a whole has a contract (for fuller discussion of this see Douglas 1976: part II, ch. 3). This sets out the 'rules of the game', as it were, and it may help to have it written up and posted on the wall for each group meeting.

(2) The basic pattern of working is for time to be negotiated or booked for particular people and pieces of work at the beginning of the meeting. Sometimes the supervisor will want to raise issues, and sometimes it will be the group members who do so. In each case, a block of time (from five minutes to half an hour, say) is arranged, and the supervisor as chair makes sure that that it is adhered to. After a few sessions, members will become adept at working out how long something needs; and the method has the advantage that it eventually undermines the 'doorknob syndrome' (p. 67) because members take responsibility for how long they want to discuss a particular item.

(3) The supervisor chairs the proceedings, and may well take an active role in working with one individual at a time, as in individual supervision. However, she can also draw on the knowledge and skill of the other participants to give new angles on things and reactions. In its simplest form,

this is like throwing the debate open to the floor, but it does need to be monitored. Whitaker and Lieberman (1965) suggest that, because of group processes, it is likely that any potential source of conflict will first generate a 'restrictive solution' from the group members, and this has to be worked through and past before an 'enabling solution' emerges. Experience indicates that, because of their often prescriptive outlook on their work, residential and day-care staff are particularly prone to jumping in with restrictive solutions at an early stage, and it can take considerable work to get past them.

(4) The work described above may be regarded as the filling in the sandwich. If we refer back to the stages in the supervision session Chapter 6, it can be seen that attention needs to be paid to the bread and butter, or else the whole thing falls apart. The first slice is the opening, which needs to include the negotiation of time not only for this session's work, but also for things carried over from previous sessions – rather like 'matters arising from the minutes of the previous meeting'. An adaptation of the proposed system of recording and monitoring (Chapter 7) may provide the material for this.

The second slice is the attainment of closure, which is all the more important in the group setting because it is harder to feel in control of what is going on than it is in the individual session. Some kind of ritual endings, such as giving members the opportunity to say anything they want to that they have not had a chance to say, or ruling that in the last five minutes everyone says something appreciative about colleagues' work, serves this purpose well.

The initial challenge of group supervision is to establish trust, because practically everything follows from that. The second step is *familiarity*, in the sense of everyone knowing what kind of meeting this is, and what they are there to do. From then on, the supervision group can become a *team*, a kind of self-help group in which the role of the designated supervisor is more like that of the conductor of an orchestra –

setting the pace and bringing people in as appropriate – than of a direct supervisor. This stage may never be reached, but it is the vision to aim for.

## SUPERVISION OF GROUPS

Supervision of groups is an altogether more complex activity than simply supervising individuals in a group setting, because it operates at so many different levels.

(1) There is the institutional or community level, in which the staff team is a microcosm of the whole establishment, including clients. What happens to staff and between them is taken to be a reflection of what is going on for everybody, and holds up a mirror to the issues in the client group (see Polsky 1965; Wills 1971; also p. 103).

(2) There is the team level, relating to the way in which the members complement each other in the working situation, their tendencies to support or undermine each other, their tendencies to pigeon-hole each other, their active disputes and passive tensions, and working norms.

(3) There is the group level, of behaviour in the meeting, which may reproduce any of the above, play variations around the theme, or even be quite different from it.

(4) There is the level of the group-and-supervisor system, to do with the way the supervisor is perceived and used by the group as a whole or by sub-groups within it.

(5) There is, as in individual supervision but writ larger, the level of the person-in-role, the individual counterpart to levels (2) and (3). Do I feel myself to be what everyone else sees me to be? Do I feel comfortable with it? Have I the space to change it if I want to?

(6) And there are the personal understandings and feelings of the members.

Any or all of these levels may be in operation at any one time, and it will depend on the discipline of the supervisor which he pays attention to. A systems-oriented supervisor may see the whole group in terms of what it says about the whole community; a humanistic psychologist might be more inclined to concentrate on the personal learning opportunities afforded by the whole to each person. No one can do full justice to the infinite variety of experience and interaction in the group, but everyone has a contribution to make. To complicate the picture further, some of what is going on may be open and above-board; some may be conscious but nevertheless covert, such as internal politicking; some may be conscious but inarticulate, in the sense that members themselves have not yet realized what it is they are doing; and some may be unconscious.

Everything that has been said about supervision in groups therefore applies to supervision of groups, with the exception of the method of individual supervision in public. But it is not possible to provide any similar recipe for supervision of groups; all that a text of this size can offer is a pointer to associated disciplines that may help, and encouragement to an intending supervisor in this field to seek extensive further training and experience. This is not to say that supervision of groups is a particularly esoteric art, or even that doing it badly is dangerous, but that working in fits and starts as the inexperienced supervisor tends to do is not very profitable in its outcomes for the establishment as a whole. Without such pay-offs in the outside world, the whole exercise tends in the direction of morbid corporate navel-gazing, which leaves staff feeling worse at the end than at the beginning.

One thing is clear, however; the constitution of the group *needs to be a working team* – all of it. Any absences lay the absent member open to all kinds of scapegoating or fantasies, and free the group to avoid awkward issues by the adoption of such tactics. Size becomes a problem here, because a working team can be relatively large; and if it is divided into smaller units (such as shifts), there is a problem about inter-group relations. However, if community meetings can be run successfully in therapeutic communities with up to one hundred members, this does not rule out staff teams of fifteen or so working together in supervision.

The supervisor will probably be an outsider, at least an

outsider to that staff team. This is because it is extraordinarily difficult, some would say impossible, for someone who is both part of the team and often a leader within it to act and think with the objectivity that is called for by supervision of groups. It is almost inevitable that an insider will be defensive in some measure about her own working contribution, and even if she can set this aside at the conscious level the energy required to do so depletes what she can give to the activity of supervision. The outsider can come from any discipline, provided that she has the relevant skills; intimate knowledge of the working set-up can be a positive disadvantage (see Revans 1972: 4–5).

The closest parallel to supervision of groups is to be found in family therapy. In residential institutions in particular, the paradigm of the family has always been very powerful and influential (Davis 1981); so it is not surprising that the discipline developed to understand the dynamics of family life and to intervene in the family system as a whole should yield plenty of ideas for the residential community. There is a tendency for supervision of groups to become precious and unwarrantedly intense; that too is reproduced in family therapy. But the best work in the field does not forget, as group-care staff should not forget, that it is in the practicalities of looking after people, such as getting meals on the table, providing a comfortable home, and day-to-day control, that the real work is done.

# 14 Concluding Unscientific Postscript

I have borrowed the title of this chapter from the Danish philosopher Kierkegaard, for two reasons. First, because in his polemic, *The Concluding Unscientific Postscript* (1846), he maintained that 'truth is subjectivity'. Very roughly, he was drawing attention to the need for integrity in the search for truth, as opposed to the idea that 'truth' is something objective, waiting to be discovered outside a person. Second, because the title accurately describes this conclusion: it is intended to draw attention to the non-scientific and non-technical considerations that are most important about supervision.

The counterpart to Kierkegaard's assertion about truth is that, in supervision, technique is less important than the values, integrity, and motivation of the supervisor. Given the right qualities, any supervisor is likely to do more good than harm – although she could probably do even more good by undertaking supervision in a planned and systematic way.

The test of the effectiveness of supervision is the experience of those who live in or use a group-care establishment. It is not possible to be 'scientific' about measuring that experience, either, and it is to a large extent an article of faith that better practice leads to improved quality of life for them. It is reasonable to suppose that there is some connection, however, although it may not be direct.

Some clients are dismayed to discover how professionalized is the task of looking after them: 'Am I such an odd person that people need training and continuing support to look after me?' But this kind of question is likely to arise only if 'professionalism' implies coldness, distance, and non-involvement on the part of the staff. Supervision that is all technique and no feeling, all head and no heart, will communicate such values to the staff, and they may be expected to reproduce them in their work and in their relationships with clients. On the other hand, supervision that embodies values of concern and respect for staff and clients is equally likely to enable staff to work in that way in their turn. Social service agencies are not noted for extending the same consideration to their employees that they encourage them to give to their clients. Such lack of concern must ultimately sap the strength of staff. Undertaken for the right reasons, good management practices and caring professional supervision can in some measure endow staff with commitment, confidence, and stamina.

These positive values cannot be adopted simply for supervision purposes; they have to be the foundation of practice at all levels. To some extent this sounds like the get-out of the old Chinese alchemist, who gave his disciples the recipe for making gold and assured them that it always worked – but only as long as one did not think of a little red monkey while using it! I am not claiming that if the ideas in this book do not work it is because somehow the supervisor's attitude is not right, but rather that, at bottom, a concern to put these values into practice is the only worth-while reason for undertaking supervision at all.

# References

Ainsworth, F. and Fulcher, L. C. (eds.) (1982) *Group Care for Children: Concept and Issues*. London: Tavistock.

Atherton, J. S. (1983) 'No Smoke without Fire'. *Social Work Today* 14 (40), 28 June.

—— (1984a) 'Never Give up on a Good Thing'. *Social Work Today* 15 (32), 16 April.

—— (1984b) 'One Step at a Time'. *Social Work Today* 16 (12), 19 November.

Bannister, D. and Fransella, F. (1980) *Inquiring Man: The Psychology of Personal Constructs* (2nd edn). Harmondsworth: Penguin.

Bateson, G. (1973) *Steps to an Ecology of Mind*. London: Paladin.

Becker, H. (1970) *Sociological Work*. New York: Free Press.

Beedell, C. (1970 *Residential Life with Children*. London: Routledge & Kegan Paul.

Berne, E. (1961) *Transactional Analysis in Psychotherapy*. New York: Grove Press.

—— (1966a) *Games People Play: The Psychology of Human Relationships*. London: Deutsch.

—— (1966b) *Principles of Group Treatment*. New York: Grove Press.

Berry, J. (1975) *Daily Experience in Residential Life*. London: Routledge & Kegan Paul.

Bettelheim, B. (1950) *Love Is Not Enough*. London: Collier-Macmillan.

Bion, W. R. (1970) *Attention and Interpretation*. London: Tavistock.

Bramham, P. (1980) *How Staff Rule*. Farnborough: Saxon House.

Brown, A. (1984) *Consultation: An Aid to Successful Social Work*. London: Heinemann/Community Care.

Brown, J. A. C. (1963) *Techniques of Persuasion*. Harmondsworth: Penguin.

Buzan, T. (1974) *Use Your Head*. London: BBC Publications.

Caplan, G. (1964) *Principles of Preventive Psychiatry*. New York: Basic Books.

—— (1970) *The Theory and Practice of Mental Health Consultation*. London: Tavistock.

Carter, R., Martin, J., Mayblin, B., and Munday, M. (1984) *Systems, Management and Change: A Graphic Guide*. London: Harper & Row.

Central Council for Education and Training in Social Work (1973) *Residential Work is Part of Social Work: A Discussion Paper*. London.

Davis, A. (1981) *The Residential Solution*. London: Tavistock.

de Board, R. (1978) *The Psychoanalysis of Organizations*. London: Tavistock.

de Bono, E. (1985) *Edward de Bono's Thinking Course*. London: BBC Publications.

Douglas, T. (1976) *Groupwork Practice*. London: Social Science Paperbacks.

—— (1983) *Groups: Understanding People Gathered Together*. London: Tavistock.

Festinger, L. (1957) *A Theory of Cognitive Dissonance*. Evanston, Ill.: Row, Peterson.

Feuerstein, R. (1979) *Instrumental Enrichment*. Baltimore, Md.: University Park Press.

Golding, W. (1954) *Lord of the Flies*. London: Faber.

Harris, T. (1973) *I'm OK, You're OK*. London: Pan Books.

Hawkins, P (1982) 'Mapping It Out'. *Community Care*, 22 July.

Hofstadter, D. (1983) *Gödel, Escher, Bach: An Eternal Golden Braid*. Harmondsworth: Penguin.

Jones, H. (1978) *The Residential Community: A Setting for Social Work*. London: Routledge & Kegan Paul.

Jones, M. (1976) *The Maturation of the Therapeutic Community*. New York: Human Sciences Press.

Kadushin, A. (1976) *Supervision in Social Work*. New York: Columbia University Press.

Kelly, G. (1955) *The Psychology of Personal Constructs* (2 vols.). New York: Norton.

Kierkegaard, S. (1846) *Concluding Unscientific Postscript to the Philosophical Fragments*. Trans. D. F. Swenson. Ed. L. M. Swenson. Princeton: Princeton University Press, 1941.

Lewin, K. (1947) 'Frontiers in Group Dynamics'. *Human Relations* I (1); reprinted in D. Cartwright (ed.) *Field Theory in Social Science*. London: Social Science Paperbacks, 1952.

Lifton, R. J. (1961) *Thought Reform and the Psychology of Totalism*. Harmondsworth: Penguin.

Mager, R. F. (1962) *Preparing Instructional Objectives*. California: Fearon.

Mattinson, J. (1975) *The Reflection Process in Casework Supervision*. London: Institute of Marital Studies.

Menzies, I. E. P. (1967) *A Case-Study in the Functioning of Social Systems as a Defence against Anxiety*. London: Tavistock Pamphlet No. 3.

Milgram, S. (1973) *Obedience to Authority*. London: Methuen.

Miller, E. J. (ed.) (1976) *Task and Organisation*. Chichester: Wiley.

Miller, E. J. and Gwynne, G. V. (1972) *A Life Apart*. London: Tavistock.

Miller, E. J. and Rice, A. K. (1967) *Systems of Organisation*. London: Tavistock.

Parad, H. (ed.) (1965) *Crisis Intervention: Selected Readings*. New York: Family Service Association of America.

Payne, C. and Scott, T. (1982) *Developing Supervision of Teams in Field and Residential Social Work: Part I*. London: National Institute for Social Work, Paper 12. (Also Part II: Six Exercises (1985).)

Pettes, D. (1979) *Staff and Student Supervision: A Task-Centred Approach*. London: Allen & Unwin.

Pincus, A. and Minahan, A. (1973) *Social Work Practice: Model and Method*. Ithaca, Ill.: Peacock.

Polsky, H. (1965) *Cottage Six*. New York: Wiley.

Revans, R. W. (1972) *Hospitals: Communication, Choice and Change*. London: Tavistock.

Reynolds, B. (1965) *Learning and Teaching in the Practice of Social Work* (2nd edn). New York: Russell & Russell.

Robinson, M. (1984) *Groups*. Chichester: Wiley.

Rogers, C. R. (1951) *Client-Centred Therapy*. London: Constable.

Shaw, Henry Wheeler (1874) *Josh Billings' Encyclopedia of Wit and Wisdom*.

Shaw, J. (1974) *The Self in Social Work*. London: Routledge & Kegan Paul.

Smail, G. (1982) *Prophecy, Behaviour and Change*. London: Routledge & Kegan Paul.

Steiner, C. (1975) *Scripts People Live*. New York: Bantam.

Truax, C. B. and Carkhuff, R. F. (1967) *Towards Effective Counselling and Psychotherapy*. Chicago: Aldine.

Tutt, N. (1974) *Care or Custody?* London: Darton, Longman & Todd.

Waddington, C. H. (1977) *Tools for Thought*. London: Paladin.

Watzlawick, P., Beavin, J., and Jackson, D. (1967) *Pragmatics of Human Communication*. New York: Norton.

Watzlawick, P., Weakland, J., and Fisch, D. (1973) *Change*. New York: Norton.

Westheimer, I. J. (1977) *The Practice of Supervision in Social Work: A Guide for Staff Supervisors*. London: Ward Lock.

Whitaker, D. S. and Lieberman, M. A. (1965) *Psychotherapy through the Group Process*. London: Tavistock.

Whiteley, J. S. and Gordon, J. (1979) *Group Approaches in Psychiatry*. London: Routledge & Kegan Paul.

Wills, W. D. (1971) *Spare the Child*. Harmondsworth: Penguin.

—— (1979) 'The Moral Perspective'. In P. Righton (ed.) *Studies in Environment Therapy: Vol. III*. Toddington, Glos.: Planned Environment Therapy Trust.

Winnicott, D. W. (1971) *Playing and Reality*. Harmondsworth: Penguin.

# Name Index

# Subject Index